How to
Sell Yourself

THE SUNDAY TIMES

How to
Sell Yourself

Ray Grose

KoganPage

LONDON   PHILADELPHIA   NEW DELHI

Publisher's note

Every possible effort has been made to ensure that the information contained in this book is accurate at the time of going to press, and the publishers and author cannot accept responsibility for any errors or omissions, however caused. No responsibility for loss or damage occasioned to any person acting, or refraining from action, as a result of the material in this publication can be accepted by the editor, the publisher or any of the authors.

First published in Great Britain and the United States in 2010 by Kogan Page Limited

120 Pentonville Road	525 South 4th Street, #241	4737/23 Ansari Road
London N1 9JN	Philadelphia PA 19147	Daryaganj
United Kingdom	USA	New Delhi 110002
www.koganpage.com		India

© Ray Grose, 2010

The right of Ray Grose to be identified as the author of this work has been asserted by him in accordance with the Copyright, Designs and Patents Act 1988.

ISBN   978 0 7494 5638 2
E-ISBN 978 0 7494 5895 9

The views expressed in this book are those of the author, and are not necessarily the same as those of Times Newspapers Ltd.

British Library Cataloguing-in-Publication Data

A CIP record for this book is available from the British Library.

Library of Congress Cataloging-in-Publication Data

Grose, Ray.
  How to sell yourself / Ray Grose.
        p. cm.
    ISBN 978-0-7494-5638-2
  1. Executives--Promotions. 2. Self-presentation. 3. Corporate image. 4. Career development. I. Title.
    HD38.2.G74 2010
    658.4'09--dc22

                                                           2009029038

Typeset by Saxon Graphics Ltd, Derby
Printed and bound in India by Replika Press Pvt Ltd

Contents

Introduction

Everyone working in an organisation has seen unworthy executives advance up the corporate ladder while more competent alternatives have been overlooked.

Why does this seemingly unfair situation occur over and over again?

It is because many dedicated and competent executives concentrate on doing their jobs to the very best of their ability but fail to promote themselves as valuable organisational members. In particular they pay little attention to a fundamentally important factor in organisational success: their personal 'image' – the picture that other people hold of them, made up from the quality of thousands of interpersonal interactions.

The 'correct' image for an individual is rarely just a projection of personality. Successful executives purposefully design, manufacture and adapt their image appropriately for their position and to the culture of their organisation. They recognise that their personal image is the most important component in others' evaluation of them.

They also understand the necessity of attending to issues of 'good' image on a daily basis and that 'selling yourself' is a function of the executive irrespective of their place in the corporate hierarchy.

This book gives indispensable guidelines on how you can sell yourself, particularly how you can develop and manage your image for success.

1

Personal image – the basis of self-promotion

When you start to consider how you are going to 'sell yourself', you need to be clear as to what you actually mean by the term 'sell yourself'. What you are going to sell is not your essence but your image. And you are not going to 'sell' your image in a monetary sense; rather you are going to promote your image as a way of advancing yourself.

Image. What it is. What it is not.

Image is not something you actually possess. Like beauty, image is in the 'eye of the beholder'. Everyone has their own image of you. It is the summary of their perceptions, subjective feelings and evaluations of you. When others talk about you, it is not the real 'YOU' they are discussing but their concept of you made up of many personal encounters with you and what others have said about you.

You might think that your personal job performance should be the main determinant of your image because your performance is important to others. Certainly how well you carry out your tasks is important to your own team leader, for you are an economic/production unit in a group that your leader is responsible for and your leader will be evaluated on the productivity of the team. Also, your immediate peers might be intensely interested in your output levels because you may be in competition with them. Or they may be concerned with your output because you all work as a team and their remuneration is related to team output. But most people in the organisation are usually only indirectly concerned about the productive/economic benefits you bring to the organisation. How they evaluate you, and therefore your image in their eyes, may be based on something surprisingly different, eg the help you can give them in solving problems, or your willingness to share some skill or knowledge of benefit to them. Even for those who rely on your job performance this may not be the main determinant of a 'good' image. For instance, they might value more highly the help you provide them in doing their own job better.

Image is not likeability. Generally in our social lives we behave in such a way that we will be liked, at least not disliked. Indeed, one of our basic psychological needs is to be liked. But in organisations likeability is usually only one of many positive aspects to image. We have all heard it said, 'He is a nice chap, but...', or 'I like her, but I wouldn't want to work for her.' Indeed, in some organisations likeability might be considered counter-productive, eg in active military groups.

This example also shows that attributes which constitute 'good' image in one organisation will differ from those in another. The 'culture' of an organisation will also be a factor in determining what a 'good' image is. You need to determine what constitutes 'good' image for your organisation and your position in it so that you know precisely what it is about yourself you are going to sell.

Why your image is so important

How you are perceived by other organisation members is fundamentally important to you because in many instances this perception will determine the way they interact with you and this will have an impact on your success, or otherwise, eg if they believe you to be disloyal and a 'clock watcher' they will not offer support for your efforts to get a better position.

Image, like reputation, precedes you. People who have not even met you will still have an image of you. They will have heard about you informally. Or, out of curiosity, they may have asked others who work with you, 'What do you think of so and so?' The reply they receive will be the basis of the image they hold of you. In this way your image is contagious.

The opinion of others is likely to be sought when supervisors make decisions concerning you. You cannot 'sell yourself'; you cannot advance in your organisation without the decision makers holding a 'good image' of you. Obviously, it is crucial that you develop and maintain the best possible image and the one most suited to your organisation.

How image is developed or changed

Every time you communicate, particularly face-to-face, with other organisational members you have an opportunity for projecting or reinforcing a positive image. It is also an occasion when, if you are not careful, you could inadvertently damage it.

This is because, even in the act of communicating some petty information, you are also displaying your attitudes, values and your potential for being of some value to the person with whom you are communicating. For instance, you might inform a work colleague that the lift is broken. You might say, 'The bloody thing is broken again. When are they going to fix the damn thing?'

Amongst other things, this brief comment might suggest to your colleague that you are negative, bad mannered (in that you use crass language – see below), and disrespectful of other organisational members (the incompetent 'they'). Your listener may not, therefore, consider you someone they should associate with. On the other hand, you might say, 'These things are sent to test us.' This might suggest that you identify with your colleague (in that you are both suffering the same inconvenience), that you have a resilient, productive attitude, and you are not distracted from your tasks by minor impediments. Obviously the second response encourages a more positive image of you. In more involving communications, such as performance appraisals, your image comes in for far closer scrutiny.

It is in your communication with others that you can let others see that you have the qualities that they find attractive and that the organisation as a whole values. You need to identify what these qualities are for your particular organisation so that, by projecting them, you can build a 'good' image of yourself and 'sell yourself' effectively.

An unfortunate aspect of 'good' image is that it is extremely fragile. Although it can take years to develop, it can be severely damaged, even destroyed, in an instant. Conscientious image developers must be particularly sensitive to how and when this could occur and protect themselves from any potential disaster.

Summary

'Selling yourself' effectively means promoting your image. Your image is not 'You' but others' perceptions of you. Your image is fundamentally important because others will make judgements concerning you based upon your image in your organisation. You can develop a 'good' image by determining what qualities your particular organisation finds desirable and then making sure that all your communication, particularly face-to-face, displays those qualities.

2

Success indicators – general elements of 'good' personal image

What qualities constitutes 'good' personal image may vary between organisations due to their different cultures. However, the great majority of organisations have basic similarities: they are hierarchical, conservative, value stability, have published objectives, etc. As a result these organisations tend to have similar ideas about what is an appropriate image for their executives. These qualities are listed below. I will label them Success Indicators.

Doing your job well

Every employee joins an organisation to do a specific job. Hopefully, this should be defined and the employee given clear performance objectives. These should integrate with the objectives of other organisation members to achieve the overall goals of the organisation. Your 'good' image will then be based on how well you carry out your actual job: how well 'you do your bit' for the overall welfare of the organisation and its members. In profit-orientated, small organisations where group bonuses are paid on productivity, your personal contribution will be highly valued.

However, it may be surprising that personal output is not always the most overwhelmingly significant component of 'good' image. Perhaps not so surprising when you realise that the profitability/success of the organisation may not be all that important to other members who value their own advancement, or their job stability, or the social benefits offered by the organisation more than your role in its profitability. There are even some organisations where high personal output is not valued, eg those where the work team encourages all members to work at a pace comfortable for all. However, in well-run organisations 'doing a good job' will be a component in your 'good' image. In these, members pride themselves on doing a good job too and admire others who share the same value.

Commitment

Similarly, most organisations value your commitment to the organisation. This is because the members generally want the organisation to survive and prosper and their material benefits to continue. Your commitment indirectly supports the stability that they value.

As many surveys reflect, most organisational members want more than just an income from their work. They want some sort of 'meaning', some affirmation that they are valuable, a sense that what they are doing is worthwhile, and confirmation that they are working for a 'good' organisation, one which treats them with respect. Your commitment is pleasing to them because it shows to them that others, in this case you, judge your organisation to be a 'good' place to work. Your commitment endorses their decision to work there and, indirectly, supports them in their search for 'meaning.'

Your commitment also parallels their commitment, and that of other organisation members. In this way it makes you 'one of them'. It promotes *esprit de corps*. It strengthens the social unity of the organisation.

Energy

Commitment is the first step. Next your image will be enhanced if you energetically involve yourself in your work and your relationships with others in the organisation. Energy and drive not only confirm your commitment, they are indicators of strength and health, of youthfulness and vitality.

One easy way to show this energy is to act energetically. When you are on view, when you are walking around the organisation, put a spring in your step. Don't dawdle. When you are on your way to work, do it with purpose and drive. Make it appear that you cannot wait to get there and get into action.

Positive attitude

When this energy can be expressed in a positive attitude it becomes a valuable component of your 'good' image. A positive attitude is infectious. Organisation members find it motivating and energising. It makes them feel good and if you can make them feel good you will enhance your image with them. Of course, your positive outlook when expressed on some matter should not be mindless. It should be based on sound judgement. The surprising thing is that even if your supportive reasoning is flimsy, and others recognise this, they will usually go along with it, because your positive attitude makes them feel good. Positive attitude has its own attractiveness.

Answering the phone provides an ideal opportunity for demonstrating your positive attitude. Answer the phone enthusiastically. Someone wants something from you. Let them know you are prepared to provide it energetically. 'Good morning. This is Fred. How can I help you?' This is well-mannered, lively, positive. If you mean it when you say it, your caller will be impressed.

Ongoing learning

A positive attitude and intellectual energy are identified in someone who involves themselves with ongoing learning. This might be the development of skills and knowledge applicable to the workplace, eg taking a management course. But even if the area of learning is not immediately relevant, eg learning a foreign language, many fellow workers will find your efforts admirable. It demonstrates that you have intellectual capacity and personal drive.

Enjoyment

Your positive attitude will be reinforced by the enjoyment you show in your involvement with your job. In the real world, your job will not always be enjoyable. You should hide negative feelings when they occur. (Hopefully this will not be too often.) But when you are truly having a good time, show it. It makes you an attractive person. It also lifts others and indirectly motivates them because it confirms to them that, even though they, personally, might be going through a rough patch at the moment, the organisation can be a great place to work, and that they have made the right decision to commit to work there.

Ambition

Most people aspire to improve themselves. Hence the popularity of auto-suggestions such as 'Every day in ever way I am getting better and better.' We all have ambitions and goals that we strive for and we can identify with others who have similar aspirations for advancement. Ambition in the workplace is a natural extension of commitment and energy. So it should be a component of your 'good' image. However, it can detract from your image if the person who observes your ambition feels personally threatened by it. So you are wise, when you express your ambitions, to do so in a low-key, non-competitive way. You are expected to have ambitions but these should not be stated in a way that suggests you consider yourself better than others. This would be disrespectful, even if it were true.

Respect

You cannot have a 'good' image without the respect of others. Generally, you cannot have their respect without your respecting them. Respect tends to be reciprocated. So showing respect for others is imperative to achieving the 'good' image you desire.

Good manners are the foundation of all respect. Everybody has heard the saying, 'Manners makyth the man', the motto of New College, Oxford, from the 14th century. Good manners include interacting with others according to social convention. You need to address people properly, and use their names. Dale Carnegie said, 'The sound of one's own name is the most welcome sound in the language.' So utilise the names of others in the organisation when you communicate with them.

The concept of good manners extends beyond formal communications. You should give others your time beyond what is necessary for doing the task. Don't be brusque; take the time to show them that you are interested in their views, emotions, family, etc. Listen. Show your concern. When you share their views, interests or values, compliment them. Sincere compliments are part of good manners.

You can demonstrate your respect for others non-verbally by utilising something very simple, but powerful: smile when you first encounter them. There is nothing more disarming and comforting than being met by a smile and, like respect itself, a natural reciprocation takes place. Smiling begets a smile. Smiling always opens communication comfortably and allows the process of mutual respect to get under way.

I once received feedback that I appeared grumpy and aloof every morning. This surprised me. I was not grumpy and did not think I was aloof. So I investigated the circumstances to see how I could improve my image. The problem seemed to be this: I started work a few hours before the others in the office. When they arrived I would already be deep in thought going about my business. But when they arrived they expected me to greet them warmly, as they did to each other, but I was not showing the appropriate enthusiasm. I was too self-absorbed. When I recognised my poor manners, I became more welcoming and smiled more genially. I heard my image improved.

Remember: Every time you communicate with others you have the chance to impress them favourably by being well mannered. By self-awareness and self-evaluation you can condition yourself to repeatedly take this opportunity to reinforce a positive image of yourself.

Dependability

Good manners extend to being dependable. If you tell someone you are going to do something, make sure you fulfil their expectations. If you cannot do so for some reason, make sure you inform them personally of the circumstances and before they are let down.

Associated with dependability is consistency. Others interacting with you expect that you will act as you have in the past. They may rely on this expectation when making their own decisions. You could undermine them by unpredictable behaviour.

When you are dependable and consistent you will gain the trust of others. Being worthy of their trust, 'trustworthy', is a compliment and certainly a component of 'good' image.

Punctuality

Dependable people are punctual. Being late for a one-to-one meeting with a lame excuse is offensive to the person you have kept waiting. It shows disrespect and sets a poor atmosphere for the meeting. It may also upset the scheduling for the other person causing them to be late for subsequent meetings that are important to them and so damaging their image. Repeatedly being late will quickly label you as unreliable.

On the other hand, always being punctual and prepared for meetings is highly regarded by others. The quality of reliability demonstrated by consistently being on time endorses your input to the meeting. Being late makes others disinclined to consider your input no matter how beneficial it might be in isolation.

I was once a partner in a financial services firm. A partners' meeting was scheduled every Monday morning at 7.00. Decisions at this meeting were handed down by each partner to their staff at meetings held at 8.00. Unfortunately, the senior partner was a late sleeper and frequently did not arrive on time, resulting in the other partners being late and not fully prepared for their own staff meetings. The top two levels of the organisation started work on those weeks in an atmosphere of annoyance and frustration. In particular the partners were angered that their image with their staff was damaged by the senior partner's tardiness and inconsideration.

Grooming

The old Latin proverb 'Clothes make the man' has been repeated throughout history so, presumably, it has some relevance to 'good' image. Whole books have been written on the subject, correlating certain types of clothing with success in the workplace. The term for this is 'power dressing'. It promotes the concept that truly successful people choose certain styles of clothing and grooming to enhance their image.

Grooming is probably more relevant in its negative aspects. For most organisations, no one will be highly successful who dresses badly, wears outlandish or unusual clothing, or who is dirty in appearance, or experiences bad breath or body odour. But it does not seem to follow that once one has achieved an acceptable level of conformity and the quality of grooming appropriate to the norms of the organisation, further attention to personal presentation will produce spectacular returns.

However, some organisations value presentation in dress more than others. A high quality of grooming is part of their culture (see Chapter 8). If you are a member of such an organisation, it is important to dress well and you must spend the time, money and effort to achieve or exceed the expected standards. Your efforts to 'sell yourself' will be wasted if you don't.

It is often important to consider not only what you wear but how you 'carry' yourself. Your deportment, the way you walk, sit, stand, etc, is noticed by others. Slouching in chairs, dragging your feet, leaning against walls, hands constantly in pockets, may suggest to some that the person behaving this way is relaxed and at ease with themself. However, such conduct annoys others. To them it suggests unconcern, even haughtiness – not qualities of an aspiring leader. Just as for grooming, there will be standards, usually unwritten, for your particular organisation. For some organisations or professions poor deportment may be of little consequence. For others, eg an army officer, it is much more important to their image. You need to determine what levels are appropriate to your organisation and then meet them.

Outside life

All organisations want their leaders to be well-rounded. They require them to be committed to their jobs but they also prefer their executives to be socially successful in their outside lives. A happy home and stable family life, sporting activities and cultural interests unrelated to the job are admirable pursuits. They indicate personal and social maturity, which is necessary to be a successful leader. Such aspects to an executive's make-up suggest stability and social poise, highly regarded characteristics in experienced executives.

Presentations

A presentation is a formal occasion when information is exchanged. It usually includes a component of influencing. Examples would be:

- **any report, written or verbal;**
- **a salesperson's presentation of a product/service; and**
- **self-promotion in a salary review, etc.**

The presentation might be given to your supervisor, your peers, your team members, customers, or a combination of all of them. When you give presentations both you and your ideas are on show. For many executives presentations might be daily activities. It is an occasion for you to improve, or reinforce your image. Developing presentation skills is crucial for almost all positions in an organisation. Preparation and practice are essential for maximum impact. (There is more detail on giving presentations on page 52.)

In effect, each time you interact with other organisation members you are giving mini-presentations. All interactions are opportunities for you to present yourself and build your image. Each 'show' needs to be managed to improve your image by showing how you can be beneficial to the people you are presenting to.

The most important presentation: introductions

The most frequent presentation you give is when you are introduced to someone. This is a great opportunity for 'selling yourself': you have a captive audience, if only temporarily, and generally you have their attention. But you only have a few moments to communicate to the person you are meeting for the first time a few things about yourself that will impress them.

It is essential that you handle the situation effectively. We all know that initial impressions are important because they are so durable. If, when meeting someone, you make a poor impression, say you seem cold and aloof – you may be caught deeply thinking about a problem – it may take many subsequent meetings to change their first opinion of you. So, as with all presentations, you need to design what you will say and how you will say it and then practise. You must be prepared. Introductions can happen when least expected.

Factors that will influence your introduction

The formality/informality of the introduction. The introduction might be scheduled to allow the parties to start to develop a working relationship. In this case, each party will need to obtain a significant amount of information about the other. Or the introduction could take place in a corridor where people meet literally in passing.

The relative status within the organisation of the parties. Sometimes you may be introduced to someone high up in the hierarchy but you are not aware of the difference at the time.

The culture of your organisation. Some organisations can be quite formal. In these the introduction will call attention to the relative status of those introduced. For organisations that have a culture of egalitarianism much less rigid behaviour is needed.

The ethnic culture in which the introduction takes place. Some cultures have rigid conducts of behaviour for introductions. Not complying would show seriously offensive bad manners.

The combinations of these factors mean, ideally, you should have a broad catalogue of introductory behaviour at your fingertips. This is not practical. But there are some guidelines that will help you to portray a 'good' image in most initial meetings:

- **Be friendly. Smile warmly. Maintain eye contact at least for the moments when you say 'Hello', or 'Nice to meet you'; whatever is the appropriate greeting for your organisation.**
- **Show respect. Stand if you are sitting. Use your best manners. 'Turn on the charm.' Use the other person's name more than once and particularly when you part. (If first impressions are important because they are long lasting, the termination of the introduction is the most important part because the other party is most likely to remember your parting impression most.)**
- **To the extent that you have time, show a genuine interest in the person you meet. Ask about what they are doing as much as your relative position allows you. If you know something favourable about the person or what they are doing, let it be known.**
- **Commit yourself to the other person, eg 'I look forward to working with you', or '(I) look forward to meeting you again later'. Or, 'Hope I can be of help to you later', or 'If there is any way I can be of help, please let me know.' By saying something like this you have laid the foundation for a relationship to develop. The other party will have the notion that you may be of help to them. (If the person is a customer/supplier, formalise this relationship-building by giving them your card.)**
- **Always think to yourself, 'The person I am meeting may one day be of great help or value to me. They may help me advance my career, become a life-time friend, or both.' Don't waste the opportunity to make a good impression.**

After each introduction make a mental note of the person, what they look like, what you learned about them. NEVER forget their name. If you are poor at remembering names, write it down somewhere, where every so often you spend a minute refreshing your remembrance of the face and the name. How often the talent of recalling names is associated with great people, eg Julius Caesar. It is a very beneficial skill to develop.

In addition, after each new meeting assess your performance. Ask yourself what you could have done better. Do this every time and your introductory meetings will become a major way of 'selling yourself'.

Exercise:
Self evaluation and improvement

1. **Ask yourself the following questions. (Don't judge yourself. How you evaluate yourself is not relevant to your image. What is important is how others see you.)**

   Are others aware that you do your job well? Has this been acknowledged by someone and communicated to others?

   Are you seen as an 'organisation' person? Or do they see you as a 'clock watcher'. Are you one of the team? Are you seen as enthusiastic in your work?

   Does anyone ever comment about how invigorated you seem?

   Are you considered as an optimist? When problems arise do others seek your help in fixing them?

   Has anyone commented favourably on the self-improvement courses you are doing?

Has anyone ever said it is fun working with you? Do others seek out your company?

Do others believe you are going to advance quickly in your career?

Do you compliment others?

Have you ever let others down by not providing something/being somewhere as agreed?

Has anyone ever complimented you on your dress? Or mocked you?

Do others know and comment about favourable aspects of your personal life?

Have you received positive feedback when you have provided information, verbally or in writing, to others?

So these are 13 skills, values or behaviour patterns – Success Indicators – most organisations would consider contribute to a 'good' image.

2. Now with the answers to these questions to help you, make an overall assessment of how good you think your image might be in your organisation. What qualities do you have, or lack?

3. Choose two people in your organisation; one who, you think, has a 'good' image and one with a 'poor' image. Now evaluate them against the list of qualities above. How do the two differ? What can you learn from these differences?

Now sell yourself

You now know the Success Indicators that you want others to observe in you. Do something about it:

1. Keep a list of them handy.
2. Review it briefly each morning before you start work. When you are travelling into work is a good time.
3. Pick one of the Success Indicators and determine how you are going to demonstrate on that day that you possess it.
4. Review the list on the way and evaluate how you went with your exercise.
5. Get into the habit of doing this EVERY DAY!

You will quickly find that it will become second nature to you to present these Success Indicators to others. As a result your personal image will grow. You will be selling yourself to those around you.

3

Getting everyone's approval

We have examined several 'Success Indicators' that are positive for achieving and maintaining a good image generally within your organisation. There are others things that you can do to 'sell yourself' (promote your image) to the different status groups within your organisation.

Those activities and patterns of your behaviour that will enhance your image with these disparate groups have in common that they satisfy certain requirements particular to that group. By understanding the specific needs of each group, you will be better able to provide for them and, as a consequence, boost your image with each group.

Your supervisors

The higher up the hierarchy executives go, the more their behaviour is directed to supporting their egos and nourishing their own personal image.

To your supervisor you are a productive unit whose output inputs to their goals. So your supervisor will be keen for you to perform your tasks effectively. But doing your job well is only part of their expectations.

Your supervisor will want you to develop your own 'good' personal image because this will reflect their management and guidance of you. Just as a well-drilled and perfectly groomed army unit on parade indicates 'good' command by those in charge, so in an organisation an executive whose staff has a 'good' image will also have a strong image. Self-interest in developing and maintaining their own image means that your supervisor will have a keen interest in yours. The more that you do to improve your image, the higher you will rise in their estimation of you.

Should you somehow damage your image, your supervisor may take it personally and be acutely embarrassed because in hurting your own image you will have injured theirs by the same argument.

As a manager, your supervisor will be evaluated on how well their team members develop generally. This will be observed in you when you expand your skills and experience and achieve higher levels of responsibility. To accomplish this you will need sound feedback and guidance. Not only will your supervisor's ego be satisfied in providing such direction, hopefully, the noticeable improvements in your capacities will be seen as a reflection on their management skills.

Your supervisor, as your organisation leader and authority figure, expects your loyalty. Your loyalty is expressed primarily in the public support you give them. Formally, this would be shown in supporting their decisions, particularly in organisational meetings involving their own superiors and peers. Informally, loyalty is seen in supporting your supervisor politically, always speaking positively of them and endorsing their behaviour. Never take an opposing viewpoint or speak badly of your supervisor – it has a way of getting back to them, which could be disastrous for you.

Your peers

What do your peers/colleagues want from you? They want assistance in doing their job, they want friendship and emotional support, but they do not want overt competition.

Peer relationships vary between organisations. Your peers may do the same sort of work that you do or you may work in a team with them. In either case they may look to you to share your knowledge and experience to help them improve their performance. If your peers carry out different functions, then they may look to you to give them your insights into how the organisation runs. Your knowledge of office politics or processes could be invaluable to them.

There are many topics your peers will not be able to discuss with their superiors or their reporting team members. But you are available. They may consider you an ally against the 'bosses'. Or, it is with you that they can share their troubles or frustrations. They may seek feedback from you on problems they are having. Or they might just be looking for friendship. You are a source of useful information and an emotional support to them. So, when you become aware of information of value to them, actively provide it to them. The more valuable the information is to them, the more esteemed you will become in their view.

Also, make yourself available to listen to their problems. This does not mean that you become 'a shoulder to cry on'. But you do want to be seen as a confidant and supporter.

Overt rivalry with your peers is inconsistent with this helping role. It may be a facet of your job that you and your peers, or some of them, are in competition for promotion or some other reward. The rivalry need not be hostile; it can be supportive and friendly. Remember, your peer could one day be your supervisor, or report to you as a member of your own team. You don't want someone who has become an enemy, due to unpleasant prior organisational battles, in either role.

Your team members who report to you

To your team members you are not only the most important person in the organisation; you actually embody the organisation. They see you as the source of everything that the organisation provides for them. Not just salary and rewards, but security and, particularly, the opportunity to develop. You are their organisational leader/mentor. They look to you as a role model and often have an emotionally dependent relationship with you.

For your team members to climb up the organisational ladder they require development at each stage. You manage them to maximise the quality and quantity of their output, but you also need to support their development with your guidance and motivation. Your members need to learn new skills and improve old ones. They expect you to show them what to learn and how to progress. They will welcome your setting development objectives with them and providing ongoing feedback on how they are advancing. Your image with them will, therefore, be directly related to how well you function as a concerned leader and effective mentor.

Your team members cannot easily learn for themselves how your particular organisation 'works': the politics; the centres of influence; the unwritten rules; and, those characteristics of image most valued in your organisation. They can get some knowledge of these through their peers but you are the expert. Providing this information wisely will enhance your image with your staff. Of course, developing your team members is one of your responsibilities. (Strangely, this may not always be specifically stated in your objectives.) How well you do this will be reflected in the image you achieve with your superiors.

The security of your team members can be threatened from time-to-time especially when changes are proposed or occur. At such times they will look to you for leadership. They want to understand what the intended changes are, why these changes are required, and precisely what effect it will have on them. If the changes pose real threats to them, they will expect you to be an advocate for their interests, to the extent that you are able.

It is especially pleasing to your team members if you are seen to proactively champion their interests, either as individuals or as a group. If, for instance, you identify an unexpected promotional opportunity for one of your team and encourage them to take it, you can assume you will be forever respected by the individual, and the team. They will 'sing your praises' and your image will be enhanced. (A 'good' image will be more quickly communicated by others than by almost anything you can say or do directly on your own behalf to hurry it along.)

External stakeholders: clients, customers, suppliers

When you interact with members of external organisations, you should consider your image with those people. They could be people to whom, on behalf of your organisation, you provide products or services. Or they could be members of government agencies. They could also be people who provide products or services to your organisation. (They may be your potential employers.)

They all have needs. Their images of you will be determined by your satisfying those needs. What do they want from you? Of course this varies for the type of relationship you have with them. Their needs could include a desire for value for money in the product/service/information you provide. They may want interactions that are efficient and with the least amount of hassle. They may want respect for their role, timely payment, friendly communication, etc.

You need to identify the principal needs of each and then you should fashion your interaction with them so that they perceive their needs are being satisfied. If you are not sure what it is that they need most, ask them how your organisation is performing for them and you will quickly discover those things that are most important to them. Regularly asking them for such feedback will not only gather helpful information it will also indicate to them your preparedness to satisfy their ongoing needs. This practice of asking for feedback will, itself, suggest to them that you are providing value and it will project a helping image.

It is important that you develop and maintain a 'good' image with these people because you represent your organisation to them. Your image becomes the organisation's image to them. Your superiors who are concerned with the organisation's image will want to know about the quality of your interaction with them. If you are satisfying the needs of these outside people well, this information may get back to your superiors and it will reflect favourably on you. But if you do badly this news will almost certainly reach your superiors, with unfortunate consequences for you.

Summary

Table 3.1

Others	What they want	Why they want it
Your supervisor/s	For you to have your own 'good' image For you to develop professionally in your role Conspicuous loyalty For you to be a good representative for the organisation	These qualities in you will reflect favourably on their management skills AND PLAY A PART IN *THEIR* ADVANCEMENT

Your peers	Assistance in doing their own jobs Your friendship/ support Access to your knowledge about the organisation	Your professional and personal support will help them do their jobs and HELP *THEM* ADVANCE IN THE ORGANISATION
Team members	For you to be a 'good' mentor Opportunities for their development Access to knowledge about the organisation For you to champion their interests	Your help in their development will HELP *THEM* ADVANCE THEIR CAREERS
External stakeholders	Smooth working interrelationships Value for service	Help them do their job

By providing each group with the opportunity to achieve what they want for themselves you will enhance your image with them.

4

Damaging your 'good' image

Obviously, executives concerned with selling themselves by developing and maintaining their 'good' image should not behave in a way that will detract from it. There are some recognised 'Don't Dos' that must be avoided. Even though such behaviour is blatantly counterproductive, it can be observed every day in every organisation.

Each executive must learn to recognise what type of behaviour is unacceptable and then energetically guard against it. Acting in a way that damages your image must be strenuously avoided. Your good image is extremely fragile: it is easy to injure, and difficult and time consuming to repair. Below are many examples of inappropriate behaviour.

Discussing third parties critically

You must assume that anything you say which is derogatory of a third party will get back to them. The person to whom you impart, in confidence, evaluations of others may not be as cautious as you are. Circumstances may occur when, unintentionally, they pass on your judgements. These will eventually get back to the third party and, as a consequence, probably bring you a great deal of grief. There is also the possibility that this person you confide in will not be so friendly to you in the future and could use the information against you.

Even if the information never gets back to the third party, you would still have damaged your image with the person in whom you have confided. They will have in the back of their minds that if you are prepared to discuss third parties with them, then you may also be willing, at some time, to discuss them behind their own backs.

It is better for your image never to say anything about others unless it is complimentary.

Gossip

You might think that a little gossip will endear you to those organisation members who get enjoyment from knowing other people's business. When they impart secrets to you they expect that you will divulge something in return. It may be amusing to be one of the gang doing something naughty or conspiratorial. Don't be tempted. The same pitfalls apply as when talking badly of others. Basically it gets down to a matter of respect for others. To discuss them with third parties, or to gossip about them, is simply disrespectful of them as individuals.

Gossiping is an insidious organisational disease. It can undermine reputations, label people inappropriately, cause serious disharmony, demotivate people and turn them against the organisation. And seriously hurt the subjects of the gossip. People who are seen as gossips are never trusted and cannot have a 'good' image.

Correcting team members publicly

A serious example of disrespect is correcting people who work for you where others can see or hear the interaction. Even correcting people for very minor things can be enormously embarrassing and belittling for the corrected person if third parties overhear. It does not help to do it in a jovial style. It can still be hurtful even if the subject goes along with the humorous way the correction is delivered.

A person publicly corrected is upset because you have seriously damaged their image. You have shown in front of others that you have no respect for the person corrected. As we have seen, respect has a reciprocal nature. You can never expect that this person will ever again have respect for you.

Even if the correction is warranted, and the person is not well liked, you will also have damaged your image with those who overhear, who will now view you as being thoughtless and insensitive – if they don't consider you callous. If the observing person is a superior, they will probably feel the need to correct you, with some embarrassment to you and a dent in your image.

Using profane or coarse language

Some people can be offended by cursing or foul language, even if they don't show it. Even people who use such language with their peers may find your use of such language to be disrespectful to them if you are their team member or their superior.

Others may be offended because your use of such language shows that you may expect them not to be offended. Even if they might not find the actual language offensive they might find your expectation about their response presumptuous.

Since such language can damage your image, and because there is no need for an articulate person to use it, avoid it.

Complaining

When you complain to others about something affecting both of you, you make the assumption that they hold similar views. If they don't hold your views, they might be offended by this presumption, or at least irked by your insensitivity. Repeated complaining on different topics becomes very irritating. Your recurring expectation of their acceptance of your view on different matters suggests that you consider them not to have views of their own and their attitude to be as negative as yours.

Constant complaining not only annoys others, by showing disrespect, but you damage your image at the same time.

Politics/religion/etc

Some people may conceal very deep personal feelings about their religious beliefs or political values or ethnic background, etc. These can be so important to them that they are central to their concept of self. Disagreeing with, or worse attacking, these beliefs can be deeply offensive to these people, even if done so unknowingly.

Even those people who openly hold views on these topics and who are quite prepared to discuss their associations and depth of commitment to their principles may take deep offence when you give an opposing or differing viewpoint. Your contrary opinion may be felt as a personal attack.

There is nothing positive for you to gain in these circumstances. You might express your respect for their views, but if at the same time you disagree with them, you do not endear yourself to them. In most organisations personal beliefs in these types of subjects are irrelevant for doing the job. It is best to steer clear of them.

Flirting

Flirting is part of daily social intercourse. It can be frivolous and flattering and quite acceptable in most social settings. The problem with such behaviour within a hierarchical organisation is that, even when meant playfully, it can easily be interpreted as more than harmless fun.

Behind all interactions between people who are on different levels of the hierarchy is the question of power. Those on higher levels have more power; those on lower levels understand that. Power is valid. It is a way of controlling behaviour and getting things done. (Later we will investigate how power should be exercised to minimise any damage to 'good' image.) Power can be used overtly, eg in giving explicit directions, or it may be used subtly by making suggestions, eg 'Do you think it might be a good idea if this were to happen?' However, it is always a feature of interactions between people on different levels. The nature of flirting is to suggest more intimate contact. If someone on a higher level flirts with someone on a lower level, the interaction may be seen to include a subtle expression of power, even if this is not intended. If the person feels that power is being exercised when they are being flirted with, and they may readily do so, they will see that use of power as illegitimate and inappropriate, and could deeply resent it being exercised on them in that way. At the least they could feel embarrassed.

If someone on a lower level flirts with someone on a higher level, the person on the higher level may feel that their position of authority is being ridiculed and feel insulted. Of course, the person might feel amused or flattered but the danger is that they will be offended.

So-called 'peers' may be on the same level on some organisational chart but they are not of equal status in their own eyes. Each will have a view that differentiates them in their own judgement from the others supposedly of the same status. Peers, therefore, could also feel offended by flirting for the same reasons discussed above.

Because flirting has the potential to damage relationships with fellow workers, whatever their level, it is better to show your high respect for them and to avoid this sort of behaviour.

Having favourites

This is most problematical with team members who report to you.

It is human nature, for whatever reason, to like some people more than others and to want to favour them in some way. However, to show personal favouritism in organisations can be very counterproductive. Those you do not overtly favour will consider that they are disadvantaged because of your bias. They will feel jealous of the favoured. All types of unwanted behaviour could result in your staff. One sure outcome is that your image will be damaged. If you happen to like some staff member more than others, hide it. Be seen to treat all team members equally and fairly.

However, you might have very valid reasons related to their benefit to the organisation that may incline you more positively to one or more of your staff. In this case your approval should be publicly based on their performance against organisational requirements and needs. You should make it clear to all your staff that your approval for an individual is not because you personally warm to them but because of what they do for the organisation and that your approval will extend equally and readily to all others who perform as well.

Losing your temper

This may be very human but it is incompatible with 'good' image. Losing your temper shows a lack of emotional control. The display of loss of control in an executive may suggest to others that the executive is weak, or deficient, and that they may not be in full control at other times, or that their decision making will always be influenced by emotional factors.

Tantrums, swearing, slamming doors, banging on the desk, screaming at staff, etc, are immature behaviours and indications of loss of complete control. They reflect badly on an aspiring executive, manager or supervisor.

Drugs and alcohol

Taking drugs may be acceptable in some quarters of society but it is a criminal or quasi-criminal offence and is totally out of place in the organisation. If you take drugs outside the workplace do not divulge it to fellow workers. The information will get around and can be used against you with severe effects.

Alcohol, the legal, almost universal, drug is more difficult. Organisational cultures vary significantly on their attitudes towards drinking, and behaviour acceptable in one organisation may not be tolerated in another. You should adjust your behaviour to match that of the more conservative of your organisation's executives. Certainly you should never appear to be affected by alcohol during work hours (social occasions at work are covered below).

More and more organisations are prohibiting the use of alcohol on the premises and at lunch. Executives in these organisations are expected to lead by example. In this environment you should abstain.

Many people have an ambivalent viewpoint on alcohol consumption. They might not excuse in others practices that they themselves engage in. As with other questionable behaviour, minor transgressions may be overlooked or explained away, but, when repeated, they damage your image. Dubious conduct tends to stick in the memory and can be used against you at some later time.

It is better to be restrained and sober and build an image of self-control and maturity.

Exercise

Ask yourself these questions:

- Do you sometimes discuss the behaviour of fellow workers with others? (Even something which seems of little importance, like what they are wearing.)

- Have you ever expressed a critical judgement about anyone at work?

- When one of your staff makes a mistake do you immediately tell them what they have done wrong when others might be able to overhear?

- Do you swear, even with your peers, even about matters unrelated to work?

- When things go wrong and it is not your fault do you complain about how unfair the situation is?

- Do you allow yourself to be drawn in when someone flirts with you?

- Do you ever slam the door or bang the doors of your desk closed or throw stuff around?

- Have you ever been inebriated at work? Or with fellow workers after work?

If you have answered 'Yes' to any of the above you are not paying enough attention to your image. Many times a day you will be tempted to act in this fashion. You cannot afford to conduct yourself this way. Observe people in the organisation who, you think, have a 'good' image. You will find they don't behave this way. Neither should you.

Now do something about any weakness

Just as with the Success Indicators we investigated in Chapter 2, it is not enough to identify your weaknesses or damaging behaviour, you must do something positive to eradicate them:

1. Make a list of these weaknesses and keep it handy. Highlight those on the list that you are prone to make.
2. At the end of each day, review your behaviour during the day against the list.
3. If you have made a mistake, think about it. Consider how you have damaged your image. Think how you have negated the productive work you have done when you have demonstrated your Success Indicators. Imagine yourself behaving differently in the future.

This self-analysis is NOT time consuming. It only takes a little discipline and keen ambition to do it every day. You will quickly find such daily self-evaluation will raise your awareness of behaviour that damages your 'good' image. Being aware will enable you to avoid it.

5

Dangerous situations

We have investigated some day-to-day behaviour that can damage your 'good' image over time. Now we shall investigate some situations that have the potential to destroy your 'good' image irredeemably.

Intimate relationships

You spend a great amount of time at work and come into contact with many people. Sooner, or later, you may find yourself attracted to someone who is attracted to you. Letting this situation develop into an intimate relationship has great potential to seriously damage your image, which is not matched with any corresponding potential to enhance it.

Let us look at a number of ways in which it could go wrong:

- **You may have a partner outside the organisation. Either keeping the work relationship secret from the partner, or facing up to the consequent difficulties of revealing the existance of the new partner, is going to be a great strain** on you and reduce your work performance and probably indirectly damage your image.

- Your new partner may inform others at work. Apart from the embarrassment, this disclosure will change your relationships with other members of staff. They might think you will favour your new partner or even conspire with him/her against their interests. They will assume that the two of you will exchange information where you would not have done so before; information given to each of you in confidence. Trust will be broken. Of course, if you have a pre-existing partner you will also be viewed as a 'lying cheat'. Disclosure can be disastrous for your image.

- Your new relationship could be discovered by accident: you could be observed in some social setting outside the workplace. Even if you had both been discreet, there are the same negative consequences of disclosure as those covered above. Added to those damaging impacts to your image, you will now also be considered 'sneaky' for previously hiding the relationship.

- Should the office relationship come to an end and finish badly, you could be open to attack from your disgruntled 'ex'. If the relationship was known in the organisation, you will look extremely foolish and be in no position to defend yourself. If the relationship was not known, you will look even more foolish, plus, at the same time, you will lose whatever trust and respect you previously enjoyed. The pain could go on and on with catastrophic results to your image. Even if the relationship ends on a friendly basis and is never disclosed, there will be left-over entanglements and distractions which could impact negatively on your performance and, as a consequence, on your image.

The only possible, but improbable, way you could enhance the image of yourself or your partner is if one of you leaves the organisation before the relationship becomes known. One of you has to self-sacrifice. Subsequent disclosure of the relationship could be positive to the image of the one remaining with the organisation. They may then be seen as a loyal and committed organisation member who respects fellow members. However, the price may be too high.

Most people in society believe that what others do in private is their own business, particularly if it is not illegal or causes harm. This tolerance usually extends to sexual behaviour. However, people's judgement changes subtly when it is someone they know who is involved in questionable activities, especially when this person's image relates to their own, however distant. In an organisation, all members are connected and there is a sense of interdependency. Team members rely on their managers for their leadership and decision making. If their leader is involved in some dubious sexual behaviour they don't judge them as immoral but they do tend to doubt their integrity and good judgement. The leader's image is tarnished.

If you aspire to success, it will be achieved more easily if you never get yourself into such a situation

Harassment

An offence against another organisational member based on religion, race, sexual preference, is so politically incorrect that, if you are guilty, your image will probably be irredeemably damaged. Even if you are not guilty, behaviour of this sort is so unacceptable that defence is extremely difficult and an accusation is likely to harm your image at least for a short time.

Sexual harassment is one of these 'inexcusable' offences. Where does flirting end and sexual harassment begin? It is very unclear. What is offensive to some, is play to others. And some people are inconsistent in their judgements; for instance, someone may be amused by behaviour towards them from a particular person, but find the same behaviour offensive from another person.

Since it is difficult to establish unequivocally what constitutes acceptable or unacceptable behaviour, clearly avoiding any behaviour that may have sexual connotations is the best course of action. The trouble is that behaviour you thought to be completely void of sexual intent or innuendo may be misinterpreted. So you need to be very cautious in what you say and do, and alert to spot any indignation, then quick to apologise and withdraw. It is no use trying to argue that your intentions were innocent; still less trying to make a joke out of it. Hopefully your obvious embarrassment at your gaff will be sufficient for minor incidents to be forgotten.

Unfortunately, because sexual harassment is in the eyes of the beholder and, with others, you are guilty before proven innocent, it is easy for someone with a grudge against you, or who has just misinterpreted your behaviour, to claim you have harassed them and to spread the accusation informally in the organisation. At least some who hear the allegation will doubt that you are blameless. Arguing your case against the accusations, if you can actually determine accurately what they are, only brings attention to yourself and could exacerbate the problem. Certainly you cannot confront your accuser.

Immediately you hear that accusations have been made against you, go to the person in the organisation who has been appointed Sexual Harassment Officer or, if there is not one, see your manager. Acting straight away to face the problem is the best thing you can do. If you wait until you are confronted, you will lose any moral 'high ground' that immediate openness may give you. Explain the situation to the Officer to the extent you understand it. Do not criticise your accuser. Take the attitude that there must be a misunderstanding. (It may, in fact, be so.) Ask the Officer for guidance and put your trust in them. Don't worry if the Officer is at a lower level in the organisational hierarchy than you – you can't do anything about it anyway. While awaiting an outcome, maintain your dignity with other organisational members. Don't condemn your accuser. Keep saying it must be a misunderstanding. Hopefully the outcome will be successful.

Unfortunately, your image is likely to be tainted, at least for a short time.

If, however, as a result, you are wrongly reprimanded, or even punished in some way, you have a dilemma: whether to fight for your good name (image) with the possibility of being judged as disloyal to the organisation, or to leave the organisation, with a cloud over your head, but with appropriate indignation.

It is really a 'lose–lose situation'. The same outcomes apply to accusations in the other areas: racial, sexual or religious discrimination. Your best course of action is to be meticulously aware of your behaviour in these extremely sensitive areas and avoid circumstances that have potential to get you into trouble.

Informal/social gatherings

These might include regular drinks after work, dinners with partners at an organisation member's home, a group going to a show. They are characterised as being relaxed, socially orientated, and aimed at having fun. These occasions have in common that the participants, or most of them, are members of your organisation. In this way they are not like the usual social gatherings that you might attend, where the reason for association is not related to the organisation and which would have participants with varied backgrounds. In this sense these work-orientated social gatherings are 'unnatural'.

Do not think that because these get-togethers are atypical that you need not worry about maintaining your organisational image. Even though the atmosphere is relaxed you are still interrelating with people you work with, so you still have to protect yourself. Indeed, for those people whom you rarely meet at work, this is the best opportunity they have to build up an impression of you. Don't let the congeniality and casual atmosphere trick you; you are still on show.

Your self-awareness and discipline may break down if the gathering includes drinking. Whatever you do, do not behave out of character. If you are susceptible to 'letting your hair down' when you have a few drinks be extremely careful. People might enjoy your being the 'life of the party' but they will also consider you unreliable if your behaviour is out of the ordinary.

Beware the 'saboteur'. In every organisation there are people who are unable to take centre-stage themselves and are jealous of those who can. Under the guise of friendly encouragement and wanting a good time for all, they urge those who start to amuse the gathering to ever-increasing levels of showing-off. These 'saboteurs' hope that those they encourage will let themselves go to the point of exhibitionism and make fools of themselves. 'Saboteurs' delight in the resulting embarrassment in others around them and the harm they have caused to the image of others of whom they are jealous. It is easy to be gradually seduced into more and more effusive behaviour by these underhand flatterers, particularly if your guard is down, as it could be in these informal, relaxed settings. So, be wary.

Christmas parties

Most social gatherings in organisations are usually well managed, reasonably subdued affairs and should not offer too much risk to those who are alert to the hazards. However, Christmas parties can be perilous.

It seems to be culturally ingrained in us that at this one time of the year we are more likely to behave abnormally. The office Christmas party is an occasion of great risk to your image. Many organisations promote an atmosphere of fun and 'bonhomie' at this event. However, some participants go too far. We all know stories of how reputations of people have been destroyed in one moment of bad behaviour. It seems that in these festive circumstances individuals, usually staid and conservative, can lose effective control and not only make fools of themselves but cause serious, irredeemable, offence. Knowing the potential for disaster that Christmas parties offer, many organisations wisely restrict them to office premises, limit their duration, and curtail the amount of alcohol available, or ban it outright. However, they cannot control what happens afterwards – these parties have a tendency to continue after the formal event.

It is not only your own behaviour that can injure your image; you can be damaged by association. Your date/partner could be someone who is unpleasant, aggressive, or sexually harassing. Or you could be the innocent object of aggression or the sexual target of another. The office Christmas party is the 'perfect', perhaps only occasion that someone with a grudge against you, or a crush on you, can express this with minimal excuse for their behaviour. Arguing afterwards that your own behaviour was blameless is difficult and probably counterproductive.

The only course of action is to attend the barest minimum you must. Make sure you have prior appointments away from the organisation environment that will remove you when this minimum has been reached. You will know when this point has been reached when the MD and/or others of the high-image executives leave. They know the pitfalls of office parties and the threat to their images. Learn from their lead.

Performance appraisals

These are the regular and formal meetings between a supervisor/ manager and their team members to assess how well the team members are functioning and developing.

Performance appraisals are usually extremely stressful for both participants and, if handled badly, can evoke all sorts of strongly negative emotions, eg disappointment, conflict, resentfulness, rage, feelings of impotence or failure, etc. There is the potential for the image each holds of the other and their working relationship to be seriously damaged, even destroyed.

This book is not the place to investigate performance appraisals in depth; however, there are a number of pitfalls which must be avoided to minimise any threat to your image. There are also opportunities to improve personal image for both the manager and the team member.

Image considerations if you are the supervisor/manager

Providing feedback on performance to one of your team is not something that should be left to the formal appraisal meeting. It should be an ongoing process. Feedback, good or bad, is more beneficial close to the time of the welcomed or undesirable behaviour. The manager should have developed the skill to identify and praise good performance without delay. Similarly, any problems or weaknesses need to be addressed when recognised – direction is a responsibility of a good manager. And where this process of providing feedback and direction happens frequently and informally, the relationship between the manager and the team member will probably be so well developed that the formal appraisal meetings will not be too stressful.

Without this level of ongoing communication, troubles can develop. The manager may identify some behaviour they dislike. If the manager does not correct it, it will recur and earlier irritation for this behaviour will grow into annoyance. If the matter is left to the periodic meeting, it may have developed into a real problem, and may become the biggest issue of the appraisal. The manager will be angry about the repeated disagreeable behaviour; the team member may resent that the manager has not mentioned it before and frustrated that it has eclipsed the better aspects of their performance. The image of each will have been damaged in the other's eyes.

Each team member wants their manager's assessment. Even though the appraisal meeting will be looked forward to with some apprehension, the member still wants it to take place according to the predetermined programme. Should the meeting be postponed by the manager, the member will feel the lack of respect this implies. It seems to the member that the manager is saying that the appraisal is not as important as whatever else is demanding attention. The manager may have to deal with something urgent, but to the team member a delay is almost a personal rejection of their needs. (It may even be that the postponement is due to the manager's inability to face any potential conflict.) The lack of respect felt by the member will incur a lessening of respect for the manager.

A performance appraisal requires agreement between both parties at the start of the assessment period about what the team member's objectives are and how these will be measured. Without agreeing to these objectives and measurement standards beforehand, the content and style of the appraisal is open to the whim or subjective assessment of the manager. Team members who had no clear idea of what was expected of them and how they would be assessed are very unlikely to be content with the outcome of poorly organised appraisals. More than likely they will resent the process and distrust their manager in the future and be seriously demotivated by the experience.

The performance appraisal is the member's best chance to assess the management skills of the manager. If the manager performs badly in the process, the manager's image will suffer badly in the eyes of the member.

Like everything else that needs to be done well, the performance appraisal requires thoughtful preparation. For the manager this may start at the commencement of the review period. The manager should keep notes on how the member performs against the measured goals and also how the member's behaviour reflects the organisation's values. (As mentioned above, if opportunities for praising or a need for correction arise, these should be dealt with immediately.) These notes will help the manager to keep a balanced perspective on the member's functioning during the whole assessment period. These continuous notes should mean that the most recent events do not outweigh previous important aspects of behaviour. The managers who use an off-the-cuff approach without notes, and who lazily dwell on more contemporary performance because it is in the forefront of their mind, will be judged as unfair, uncaring and poor managers by their team members.

This note-taking discipline should not only result in a perspective covering the whole of the evaluation period, it should also ensure that the manager will provide a balanced view including both desirable and less desirable aspects of performance. The 'halo effect' is a well-known psychological phenomenon. It refers to the fact that we do not usually think of people in mixed terms: if we assess the basic quality of a person in a positive way, we are more likely to describe their other qualities as positive. The opposite seems to hold true too. The manager/supervisor's ongoing notes should achieve a more analytical judgement of team members and encourage comment and consideration of both welcome and unwanted behaviour.

The appraisal should first address performance that has reached the required standard. It might include the bulk of the team member's tasks. If the preset standards have been reached, the performance should be recognised and praised. The sense of achievement resulting from this well-earned praise will strongly motivate the member. The manager may then be able to suggest methods of doing the basic tasks even better and ways of developing the knowledge and skills of the member.

Poor managers understand that their responsibilities include developing their team members but reckon that this development will best be achieved through correction. So they dwell on negatives and try to eliminate the weaker aspects of their member's performance. Of course, this must form part of the appraisal, but it should not dominate. No individual wants to be presented with only a list of 'to improve'. It is too demotivating. Team members want more than this and feel that they deserve it.

Praising achieved standards motivates and sets the atmosphere in which development can be planned. The development objectives and how they are to be measured for the ensuing period of assessment must be set in active collaboration between the manager and member. In this process the manager must allocate adequate resources – actual training, time diverted from other activities, etc – and the team member must clearly understand what is wanted and make a commitment. Done correctly, this consultative process can be highly motivating for the member and greatly augment the manager's image in their eyes.

This cooperation displays the right tone for the performance appraisal, which is not an occasion for the manager to dominate team members. Obviously the appraisal is a statement of power because the manager is in control and is making the assessment. But the proceedings need to be handled tactfully and sensitively because the manager is assessing the member's work effort, commitment, skill levels; in fact, everything that the member offers to the organisation. The member's cumulated inputs are an expression of their worth to the organisation and self-worth in general. How these inputs are judged is intensely and personally important to the member. If the manager is overbearing, domineering, insensitively talking about themself, then the manager will be regarded as inappropriately satisfying their own ego needs. This crass behaviour will be unhelpful, even insulting to the team member who is supposed to be the central figure in the appraisal process.

However, towards the conclusion of the appraisal meeting there is a point in time when the manager may appropriately solicit feedback on their own management skills. It is valid for the manager to ask how their interaction with their members can be altered to effect an improvement in the team member's performance: what the manager is doing, or is not doing now, which if changed would assist the team member in doing their job. This is a hazardous ploy that could open up the manager to attack. However, if the manager's attitude is sincere, the requested feedback is likely to be provided in a productive spirit. This momentary role reversal will be highly regarded by the team member, and if it should result in changes to the manager's behaviour beneficial to the member, then it will greatly enhance the manager's image.

Image considerations if you are the one being appraised

The performance appraisal also provides the opportunity for team members to strengthen their image with their manager, or weaken it.

As for everyone in the organisation, good preparation for a formal event is a 'must'. As discussed above, the conscientious manager will have prepared notes on your performance through the assessment period. These will be prepared with reference to the objectives and measurement standards agreed between the two of you at the start of the period. You should prepare similarly. You should also list how you think you have performed against your objectives and back up your self-assessment with examples of actual behaviour or actual measurement standards achieved. A comparison of your manager's notes and your own should provide a basis for discussing your performance. The quality of your preparation will reflect your professionalism and earn your manager's respect.

Your preparation should cover your past performance but it should also consider the future: what additional responsibilities you think you could take on; what career paths you see for yourself; how you think you might benefit from extra training; and what new experiences would be beneficial to your advancement. These suggestions for your future and your readiness to expand on them should demonstrate your commitment, energy and ambition – strong attributes in a staff member.

Even though your preparation is thorough, you should assume some disappointment will occur. Your evaluation of your own performance might not match that of your more experienced manager. And your plans for personal development might be too grandiose for your manager's liking. Your response to disappointment should not include obvious frustration or anger. Any loss of composure could be seen by your manager as immaturity and reduce the image augmented by your preparation. Arguing or attacking your manager's evaluation might lead to confrontation and, inevitably, you will be the loser.

So in summary, the performance appraisal is highly stressful to the participants and can result in a wide range of negative emotional states, including a loss of respect between the manager and team member. The possibility of bad outcomes can be reduced by recognising the potential dangers and guarding against them. However, if handled well, and with goodwill on each side, the outcomes can be positive, motivating and rewarding.

Arguing

The struggle of conflicting ideas is a constant dynamic in organisations. It is an essential part of decision making. The ability to reach decisions is a basic skill of executives. Not only is the quality of ultimate decisions important to the image of the responsible executive, but also the manner in which these decisions are reached.

An idea must be able to stand the scrutiny of senior management, board members, unions, clients, etc. Each idea should be thoroughly tested by debate between interested or opposing parties. Open, informed debate that concentrates impersonally on the issues is the ideal. However, between ambitious, ego-driven executives, the struggle of ideas can often break down and become a polarised dispute and a battle of contesting personalities. Impersonal debate may degenerate into rancorous argument.

Arguing has a component, even if well veiled, of attacking the individual as well as their ideas. Decisions may still be reached through arguing but the costs are high. In decisions made this way, there are winners and losers and the image of both is usually damaged in the process. Both are seen to have lost emotional control by not maintaining the debate on an impersonal level. Both parties have also demonstrated a lack of respect for each other. The winner may hurt their image with a condescending attitude, the loser by an ill-tempered defiance. The organisation may lose by the decision not being the best, and because the ongoing ill feeling may damage morale. So in considerations of image, arguing has no real winners. It is better for the executive aspiring to be successful not to become involved in it.

However, if you are the manager or the chair of the decision-making body, you can manipulate a situation that is in danger of becoming an argument, for the benefit of your image. If you can halt the degeneration by your direction, you will be looked upon as a skilled decision maker, which is very good for your image.

One way of doing this is to remove the opportunity for personality clash. This may be done by getting the conflicting parties to adopt their opponent's viewpoint in the debate. This focuses attention on the decision to be made and diminishes the opportunity for personal point scoring. Another technique is to reach a group decision using a secret ballot. This promotes commitment to the final resolution.

In conclusion, some dangerous situations, like the office affair, can be so potentially damaging to your image that the best course of action is to completely avoid them. Others, which must be faced, such as performance appraisals, require an appreciation of how they can go wrong, so any potentially harmful behaviour can be avoided.

Summary

Hopefully, you will already have decided to establish a daily routine that will dramatically enhance your image by adopting Success Indicators and by eliminating damaging behaviour. The awareness of how your image can be affected by these simple everyday situations should also extend to the more complex and less frequent circumstances where incorrect behaviour can shatter all the achievement in improving your image painstakingly made on a daily basis.

Fortunately, you can foresee most of these circumstances and prepare your responses in advance either to avoid their pitfalls or control your behaviour in a disciplined manner. When social gatherings, Christmas parties (or similar) or performance appraisals are coming up, be sure to revise the relevant sections above. Avoid intimate relationships and arguing and never act in a way that could be construed as harassment.

6

Five ways to actively self-promote

We have looked at defending your 'good' image from some damaging and dangerous behaviour. Fortunately, there are a number of ways you can actively boost your image.

Public speaking

The ability to speak fluently and confidently before groups of all sizes is an admirable skill in an executive. It is also an efficient and effective way of enhancing your image. The occasion for orally disseminating information to others, of giving a presentation, or for farewelling a member of staff, provides an executive with an opportunity to develop their image, providing the speaking is done well.

Many executives fear this situation. They are afraid their anxiety will be communicated to their audience and they will perform poorly, making themselves look foolish. Indeed, speaking before others is one of the most common phobias. Luckily, good public speaking is a skill that can be acquired by almost everyone. As with other skills, what is needed is training and repeated practice. And this is readily available from many teaching institutions or organisations such as Toastmasters.

Developing a 'good' personal image can take a long time and it relies on the haphazard and uncontrollable efforts of others to communicate it around the organisation. But speaking before others allows the executive, personally, to directly demonstrate without self-reference many of the characteristics of 'good' image already identified, such as commitment, drive, positivity, etc. Speaking before others is a powerful tool because it is usually emotionally involving for the listeners and therefore memorable, and it is efficient because the executive impacts on many listeners at the same time.

'Good' public speaking is marvellous for image, easily learned and perfected, and one of the few ways you can promote yourself without painstakingly working on your day-to-day interactions with others. For executives aspiring to success – and who is not? – it is imperative.

Giving 'good' presentations

Giving a presentation is probably the most frequent instance of public speaking in an organisational setting.

A 'presentation' is an occasion for information transfer. It usually has a component of persuasion. The presentation could have a goal to get the listeners to agree in some desired action. Examples include:

- **putting forward a new business strategy to other organisation members;**
- **proposing a new product/service to a customer;**
- **convincing your manager to increase your salary;**
- **outlining the benefits of proposed change to the customary way of doing things.**

Because 'presentations' are so common, and such an important way for you to enhance your image, it is worthwhile to consider some of the features of a 'good' presentation:

1. Each presentation has a purpose. It may be to educate, to inform, or to get the listeners to do something. You must be very clear what your objective is. You will better focus on your objective if you write it down.
2. Your image is at stake. You must do the necessary preparation. This will require planning how you are going to deliver the underlying information to achieve your objective.
3. Your preparation should also include practising your delivery. 'Role playing', ie a rehearsal, before people who can provide feedback on your performance is best, but, if not readily available, then, at least, you should role play in your imagination.
4. Your presentation must include a clear statement at the start outlining why you are talking to the listener/s. Is it to provide information; is it to get a decision? What is the goal? The listeners must know why they are devoting their time to you. The best situation is when you indicate to the listeners how the time spent will be of benefit to them. If they see a benefit they will commit their time and attention and may be more open to change.
5. Each presentation needs a beginning: when you tell the listeners what you are going to tell them and why. It needs a middle: when you actually tell them. Then an end: when you tell them what you have told them. This is not as silly as it sounds. Repetition is an important technique in getting your message across in public speaking.
6. The information should be made as simple as possible. The presentation is not an occasion to demonstrate your detailed, or technical, knowledge. If it is necessary to convey intricate knowledge do this in a handout. Adjust the level of the speech to the least informed of your listeners. Be careful, with your familiarity with the subject matter, that you don't pitch the level too high and make it difficult for your listeners to follow.

Don't use jargon or acronyms, which, if the listeners do not understand, they will find distracting and annoying.

7. At the end check with your listeners that the goal has been achieved. Thank them for their time.

People in organisations give presentations every day. If you want to have a 'good' managerial image, then make sure your presentations are high quality. Follow the above suggestions each time you give one. Remember 'practice makes perfect'. And each time you give a presentation, critically assess your performance and identify your weaknesses to eradicate them in the future.

The nasty word

Giving presentations with the purpose of getting the listeners to do something has a particular name: selling. For many, 'selling' has unpleasant associations. The 'second-hand car salesman' and the 'flashy insurance salesman' are looked down upon because, supposedly, they use underhand techniques and personal pressure to 'make' us buy something which may not be what we need. Such stereotyping has given 'selling' a bad name. Yet we all interact with others every day in circumstances where we want them to do something for us, or they want us to do something for them, ie we are involved in the selling process in either the role of the seller, or the buyer. (Indeed you, the reader, do not have this hang-up. That you can appreciate the need to 'sell yourself' is demonstrated by reading this book.)

Since we are involved in 'selling' every day, not the least at work, it should be an interpersonal process that we know lots about. But because of its bad connotations 'selling' has not generally been considered a skill in which we should be trained.

Every time you interact with another member of your organisation you have the opportunity of enhancing, or damaging, your image. Since many of these interactions will involve you in the role of seller, or buyer, you should understand the dynamics of the selling process so that you can get the most out of these interactions for your image.

'Selling', in general, is a learned skill. There are numerous courses available and books and DVDs of the self-help variety devoted to the subject. Unfortunately, the way in which these are marketed is often representative of the values, or style, we find unattractive about the stereotyped salesmen, so be selective. You should discover many ways of learning how to influence people without endangering your image. Hopefully, this book will show you some ways of selling a most important product: yourself.

The morning welcome

We have already talked about the need to respect others in the organisation and how good manners are indicative of that respect. You don't need to show your respect reactively. Each morning you have a valid reason to proactively welcome others into your day with a warm greeting. A hearty 'Good Morning, Fred', backed up with a friendly smile, will make the recipient feel good about himself and like you for it. Doing this every day to all those around you at work, tailoring the welcome to the recipient, can have an enormous positive impact on your image. It is simple but amazingly powerful.

Smiling is our natural way of acknowledging people when we meet. Once in the morning is not enough, you should develop the habit of smiling each time you have eye contact. If you don't, others could judge you as grumpy or anxious and, as a consequence, feel uncomfortable when you come into their 'space'. This unwanted effect may be completely unintentional. You may be absorbed in thinking about some problem or other, and not reflect that others appreciate a reassuring smile. But they do. And if you rarely provide it, you will quickly develop an image you don't want: grouchy, or cold. Your impact will be much more positive if you simply smile.

Step forward

Many executives come from family or social backgrounds that value very reserved personal behaviour and decorum. In an effort not to be seen as pretentious or bragging they can become modest to the point of risking being judged as meek and reserved. Such self-effacing behaviour can become a habit and the person can become uncomfortable in putting themselves forward. Too much modesty can suggest they are lacking in self-confidence and assertiveness. These are not the characteristics of a successful executive. Even if you are a naturally shy person you must overcome this and develop a personal image of confidence and self-assuredness.

One way of putting yourself forward is to offer creative suggestions. Just because things have been done in a certain way in the past does not necessarily mean that the old way has been the most efficient or effective way of doing it. You may identify a new and better way. Think deeply about your alternative. If you think it is a significant improvement then present your idea to the appropriate person, most likely your supervisor. Don't be hesitant. Even if your supervisor sees its limitations they will still see whatever merits there are to the idea and a good manager will take the opportunity to develop you by spending time explaining its shortcomings. More positively the idea might be so useful that it will be adopted – a real feather in your cap. Either way you will be seen as a committed and energetic contributor to the success of the firm.

Another way of promoting yourself actively is to volunteer. In all organisations situations arise where something unexpected needs to be done and there are not spare resources to devote to it. Offer to undertake the task yourself, even if this means working some extra time. You need not be seen as toadying to your supervisors. Say that you see the need for something to be done and explain that by not tackling the task now it will only make more work for you in the future. People will appreciate your sacrifice and remember it. But don't volunteer all the time. Your own output will suffer. And others will rely on your preparedness to put yourself out and take advantage of it.

Importantly, 'Don't hide your light under a bushel'. If you have a skill or certain experiences and they are relevant to your work, let them be known. You cannot expect others to know all about you. If you receive praise for some achievement, accept it graciously. Don't be overly modest or retiring. Be proud of your success and let others know that you are.

I remember once at an after-work gathering one of my staff telling us that he had an outstanding success with one of his accounts. He let us know, with some pride, of his achievement. My initial, unthinking, reaction was to judge him as a boaster. But as I listened I realised he was not bragging just informing us of something we really should know about. Without his telling us, I might never have known of his personal success or have learned from his experience and have trained other staff to apply his approach in other similar circumstances. I certainly remembered his contribution, which only came out because he did not 'Hide his light under a bushel'.

Summary

At the least, 'selling yourself' requires day-to-day concentration on promoting a 'good' image and eliminating behaviour that detracts from it. But your image can really be boosted if you display your skills, talents and commitment publicly in front of others. Such exposure requires self-confidence, which is innate for a fortunate tiny minority. Luckily for those who do not have it naturally it can be acquired by practice and preparation.

Speaking confidently and knowledgeably in front of others is the most important way an aspiring executive can sell themself. If you want to be a winner you must learn how to do it well.

7

Selling yourself as you climb the executive ladder

As aspiring executives rise in the hierarchy, they acquire more responsibility and power. As a result of this expansion, their need to 'sell yourself' takes on subtle new dimensions.

Power for an executive is the ability to bring about change. The higher an executive's position in the organisational hierarchy the more sweeping and encompassing are the changes they are authorised to bring about. Because these changes can dramatically impact on the lives of members, those with power are closely observed. Their image is assessed against the power they can exercise. The more power an executive has the more comprehensive are the expectations concerning their behaviour.

Staff can become angry or resentful, especially if the employment of this power feeds the ego of the decision-making executive at the expense of their staff's self-esteem.

Legitimate and respectful use of power

In accepting employment we tacitly recognise the authority of those executives who manage us. However, we expect that they will use their power legitimately, ie they will exercise their power in accordance with the objectives and rules of the organisation, not for their own benefit, ego or self-promotion. A legitimate use of power might be the promotion of a deserving team member. An illegitimate use of power would be for a manager to direct a team member to provide a personal service to them, eg picking up their kids from school. When power is exercised illegitimately like this we can rightly feel aggrieved.

When power is exercised 'over' us, particularly where we have no or little input to the decisions affecting us, we may experience a feeling of impotence. So not only should power be used legitimately, it should also be done in such a way to support the self-respect of those being directed. We do this in our general interaction with others, as a matter of manners. When we want someone to do something for us we say, 'Would you mind doing such and such?' We don't order, we request. Or, 'Do you think it would be a good idea if...?' Here the required action is made to appear as the initiative of the one being asked. In both these cases the person who is to carry out the activity is placed in a situation where they have the ability (the power) to say no. Not that this is likely. The 'game' has been to make the person carrying out the activity feel good about doing it. At the same time the person doing the requesting demonstrates respect for the person carrying out the request.

Similarly in the organisational setting, the manager should couch directives in the form of a request. This shows respect for the team member and the manager's request cannot be interpreted in any way as an attempt to demonstrate dominance by an arbitrary exercise of power.

In some instances requests may seem inappropriate. Closer to a directive might be if the manager were to say, 'I would like it if we could...' or 'It might be a good idea if we...'. In the former they are ostensibly appealing to the team member's willingness to please. In the latter they are asking the member to accept what they are proposing as worthwhile. In adopting either, managers put themselves in the same position as the team member because the directive is seen to apply to both when they use the term 'we'. If there is a negative reaction, the manager might defer the matter to a more opportune time in order to evade any confrontation.

It may take some time but if the desired action needs commitment, the manager may need to 'sell' the idea, ie the manager needs to demonstrate to the team member why the required action is beneficial to the organisation or the member and their role in it. Spending the time with the member to show the benefits demonstrates strongly the manager's respect for his member and their position.

Only in very serious circumstances, perhaps when a team member has repeatedly refused to respond to the 'request' approach, should an executive resort to explicit directives. The problem with an 'order' is that it is a 'win–lose' situation. What happens if the directive is rejected? Good managers don't let situations deteriorate to such an extent.

The point is: in making changes and getting things done through the assistance of others, the manager should generally exercise their power in such a way that their team member's sense of impotence is minimised. If this means the manager needs to take a little more time, or needs to not rely on their organisational status, then this is the way it should be done. The benefit for the manager in demonstrating respect for staff members by exercising power in that way is that the manager's image will be greatly strengthened. Respect for team members will result in a return of respect and loyalty to the manager.

Handling criticism

Executives want to have a 'strong' image. A component of this is the ability to make the tough decisions (as we will see below). Another attribute of a 'strong' image is the ability of the executive to deal appropriately with criticism. How you deal with criticism depends on where it comes from and what motivates it.

In general, however, your first response when criticised should be to take it seriously and assume it is meant in good spirit. It is a stressful thing to criticise someone and the person criticising you may not express themselves as fully or as clearly as they would in an unstressed state. So listen to the criticism attentively and explore it, by questioning, to determine accurately the nature of the criticism. Your behaviour in taking the criticism seriously shows your respect for your criticiser and their ideas and boosts your image. It shows your personality is strong enough to accept the possibility that your actions or behaviour need improvement in some way. This strength would not be demonstrated if you behaved defensively and rejected the criticism immediately and indignantly.

If the criticism comes from your superior you should not only listen to it, but assuming it is valid, you should do something about it. Determine with your manager's input what you are going to do to improve the situation. Later, with your manager, review your progress. Your preparedness to accept criticism and change your behaviour as a result will enhance your image with your manager.

If the criticism comes from a peer, listen thoughtfully. The feedback may be valid or invalid, malicious or well meant. How you react depends on the combination. You may also decide to do nothing. Either way, thank your peer for the information and then subsequently consider your options. Don't try to explain away your behaviour straight away, you will probably get into a disagreement that will only make you appear defensive and which may put the well-meant criticiser offside and please the malicious one in having disturbed you. If you judge the criticism as valid, you may feel a need to make a considered reply at a later time, but you don't have to. Agreeing to a peer that improvement is needed may be too galling for you. It may be better to let a change in your behaviour be your reply.

If the criticism is from a team member who reports to you, again thank and consider. Even if the feedback is invalid and cheeky, don't lose your composure. Think about the best course of action that will enhance your image with your team member. If it is in any way malicious, the best response may just be to ignore it. At least the critic will know that they have not been able to faze you and will admire you for your composure.

Criticism *per se* from whatever quarter is not necessarily damaging but it may be if you handle it defensively. More positively, criticism may provide an opportunity for you to demonstrate character and control, attributes appreciated in the aspiring executive.

Dealing with conflict

With team members reporting to you

In every organisation, personal and even group objectives can never be so well aligned to the overall organisational objectives that there is not occasional conflict. As well as these 'valid' conflicts there will always be interpersonal clashes. In resolving these disputes an executive may need to use their organisational power. The manner in which an executive uses their power with these two types of clashes will greatly impact on their image.

'Valid' conflicts often arise over priorities or scarcity of resources. For example, assume that two groups reporting to our aspiring executive are expanding in personnel and need new space. There is only so much available and each appeals to the executive for that space for their own group's needs. The dispute may become heated as each group's leader pushes their group's case. The executive is in a difficult position. Whatever results, it seems that at least one of the groups is going to be dissatisfied. How should the executive act?

The executive should firstly become thoroughly familiar with each group's argument for the space. A compromise solution may not be available. Then the executive should seek some creative resolution that has not occurred to the combatants: 'looking outside the circle'. Assuming that such a solution does not exist, the executive may have to decide one way or the other.

Whatever the decision, the executive should explain why it is the best one for the organisation, that the decision is not 'personal', and that the executive will continue to try to satisfy the needs of the disappointed party.

So long as the executive has been diligent in their decision making and seen to have been, and has been impartial and seen to have been, the decision should be respected and their image should not have been tarnished.

Sometimes conflict arises between parties that may seem to be 'valid' but which are really interpersonal clashes. The executive is 'used' by the combatants not for their problem-solving skills but as a weapon in their interpersonal war. Each party wants the executive's decision to favour them because it means that the decision has gone against their adversary. This is a tricky business for the executive looking to maintain a good image. The party the executive favours will think the executive is easy to use; the disadvantaged party will be aggrieved and think the executive has been duped by the other. The executive's image will suffer whatever is decided.

The executive can handle such a conflict as if it were 'valid' and ignore the interpersonal component. However, their image will suffer. Or the executive can confront the underlying problem of team-member rivalry. This will mean the executive has to point out to one or both party that there is a defect in their behaviour. This may cause some resentment. The conflict may seem to be resolved but it will really only go underground. If it is not too serious everyone may just learn to live with the underlying problem. But if it resurfaces again the executive may have to use their power. A structural change may be necessary; one where the warring parties no longer come into significant contact. In this unpleasant outcome, the executive will not have enhanced their image.

With peers

Conflict with peers in organisational life is natural and inevitable. It is not necessarily a bad thing. The energy generated during conflicts may often be productively manipulated to find creative and constructive solutions. But your image with your peers and your image generally may suffer if you don't deal with the conflict successfully. The trick is to identify situations of potential conflict early, and to be prepared to handle them with a predetermined approach.

Conflict may be viewed as a point along a spectrum stating with 'differing viewpoints' and ending with 'fight'. Movement along the spectrum can be characterised by a decrease in logical content and an increase in emotional content. Interaction at the early stages may be described as rational, fair, open and respectful. But unless a solution is quickly found the situation may deteriorate and become increasingly personalised, aggressive, defensive and stressful. It is the diminishing respect that is the threat to image. As may be expected, the opportunity for reaching a solution without a loss of self-image for at least one of the parties diminishes the further one goes along the spectrum towards 'fight'.

Power may become involved in disputes with your peers. Your superior may assert their authority and impose a solution to the conflict. As we have seen, this is a legitimate use of power by the manager. Good leaders will make correct decisions and hopefully, make the experience a positive and learning one for their team members. But conflicts may arise between people of similar status or between groups of similar influence where resolution is better handled without higher management involvement.

The executive aspiring to success should have before their mind ideals of how to behave during conflict resolution that will

minimise any loss of respect between the conflict parties. The
executive should also have ready a list of procedures to propose to
assist solving the problem.

Behaviour demonstrating respect

- **Face the conflict without delay.** Problems don't usually go
  away. The longer they are left without resolution the
  more annoying they become and the more difficult they
  are to resolve. Meet and discuss, 'like adults', as soon as a
  problem is identified. Accept that the problem is shared,
  'We have a problem.'
- **Clearly understand each other's viewpoint.** Without
  proposing solutions, each party should, without
  interruption, state their case. (Even better would be to
  state the other's case.) This could be done in writing
  before the problem is thrashed out.
- **Don't be personal.** Assume goodwill on the other side.
  Label both of the conflicting viewpoints as reasonable and
  rational. Praise the other's behaviour as helpful and their
  possible solutions as constructive. Identify their good
  points. Look at all proposals as subjects for analysis, not
  as something 'owned' by the proposer. If it helps in
  reaching a solution, let the solution be 'theirs'. Your
  magnanimity will enhance your image with your peer.
- **Be patient.** Solutions don't come instantly. Perhaps
  further analysis of the problem is required. Keep your
  composure, don't get frustrated and angry. This will
  impede your rational approach.
- **Keep communication going.** When you reach an impasse
  stop before you both become irritated. Adjourn but set an
  agreed time to renew the process. This gives both parties
  the opportunity to think unemotionally about the
  problem and to consider the other side's now clearly
  stated viewpoint.

Procedural suggestions. There are a number of techniques that may assist in achieving resolution without ill feeling:

- **Agree on an approach. After each side's viewpoint has been made clear, before trying to reach a solution, it may be a good idea to agree on what approach you are going to take. Agreeing on how you are going to go about solving the problem sets a good foundation for actually solving the problem. This strategy sets a tone of goodwill and provides a structure for resolution.**
- **Identify points of agreement. When you start to analyse each other's viewpoint, start by finding items common to both. This will show that you are not 'attacking the man'. As a result both sides should become less defensive and more productive.**
- **Take the other's side. Try arguing each other's case. This may give you insight into the problem; at least is will ensure you understand the other's viewpoint. It may become humorous. Great. Laughter is a good stress reliever and promotes goodwill.**
- **Try a mediator. Another peer, unconnected with the problem, could be invited to help. The mediator might be 'active' and in this case could suggest solutions. Or 'passive' where the role would be limited to ensuring no personal attacks, and focusing on common ground and a joint solution.**

Conflict with your superior

As with all conflicts, bring them out into the open as soon as they arise. Obviously you are not in a situation in which you can use power to solve a problem with your superior/manager. Rational argument should be your approach and hopefully, it will be the manager's too.

You will not necessarily damage your image in your manager's eyes by bringing up the problem, but you may, depending on how you behave. The more emotional you become, the less self-control you will seem to have. Throughout the process of solving the problem you should appear relaxed, composed and rational. When a decision is reached, should it go against you, don't show any reluctance to go along with it and don't be seen to hold a grudge afterwards.

Crisis management – the tough decisions

Executives aspiring to success may at some stage in their career have to put a decision into effect which will mean cutting back rewards or even reducing staff. Tough decisions are those that result in pain to others. Executives are generally reluctant to make tough decisions but circumstances may give them no choice. How does an executive do this with the least damage to image?

It is appropriate for the executive to show concern for those who are hurt and to do whatever they can for them. However, executives have responsibilities to the organisation and, although they may be agonising over the injury being inflicted, they must appear to be firm and resolved at the same time. They also have a responsibility to those hurt to explain the reasons to whatever extent they are able. This should have the result that their decisions are seen as unavoidable.

Hopefully, then the executive will be seen as both caring for the individuals and loyal to the organisation, attributes which do not damage a 'good' image. Also, handling tough decisions sensitively and with personal composure will be viewed as a strong management quality.

Recruitment

Executives exercise obvious power when they choose between applicants for a job. If a good decision is made and the applicant turns into a valued organisational member, the decision to hire that person will probably not be remembered. However, if the applicant chosen by the executive turns out to be unpopular, the new person will be a constant reminder to other members of the organisation that the executive made a poor decision and they will be living evidence that the executive has substandard interpersonal skills.

Since there is little to be gained, and potential for long-lasting damage to their image, executives who realise they have little talent when it comes to judging people they don't know, tend to give recruitment tasks to others.

If a recruitment job is unavoidable, the best option for executives who realise their limitations is to bring in others to assist in the recruitment process; a bad joint decision is far less damaging to the executive's image than one made alone.

If the new applicant turns out to be a good organisation member whether chosen by the executive alone or in a group, the executive can still get a bit of the credit. Because the executive has hired the popular new member, the executive has a justification for assuming the mentor role with their 'protégé'. This association will remind others that a good decision has been made and this will reflect favourably on the executive's image.

Taking the next step up

Moving up the organisational ladder becomes harder and harder the further you go. There are fewer places, the competition is fierce and your opposition is of a higher quality. You are not 'selling yourself' in a vacuum. You are promoting yourself against other contenders. You want to win that job, but you don't want to damage your image in the process.

Desirable positions become available when the incumbent moves on, or new positions are created through expansion or corporate restructuring, or you might see how a new position would be advantageous to the organisation and suggest it.

Whatever the reason, aspirants for the position might be from within or external.

What you can do to maximise your chances

Hopefully, the best thing is what you already have in train: 'selling yourself' generally as you have learned to do from the ideas above.

Extra efforts you can take

Thoroughly familiarise yourself with the nature of the job. Assess your strengths and weaknesses for the position. Develop a presentation to the decision makers that will show them how they and the organisation will benefit by choosing you. Then be proactive. Don't wait for submissions of interest to be requested or for the job to be advertised. You make the approach as soon as you can. Make it easy for the decision makers to decide on you and not go through the tedious and dangerous task of selection. (Make sure to include in your proposal how your vacant position can best be filled.)

What if your peer/s are competitors for the position? To what extent should your presentation include your arguing that you would be better suited to the job?

This is tricky. You want to be seen as aggressively seeking the position, but you may not want to be seen as stepping up on the heads of your fellows. On the other hand, you also don't want to be seen as being too considerate of peers when the new position may require a level of ruthlessness. (On a practical level you don't want to attack a peer who might win the job and be in a position of influence over you, or with whom you will have to continue to deal should neither of you get the job.) It is at times like these you really need to have an in-depth knowledge of your organisation's culture (see Chapter 8).

The best course of action is one that treats your colleague in competition with respect. In your presentation do not concentrate on their deficiencies or weaknesses for the position. Rather present their qualifications and strengths for the position. Do this fairly and dispassionately. Then present your own. Especially identify the key requirements for success and demonstrate how well you fill these requirements. This process has a particularly attractive facet to it from the point of view of the decision makers: should you get the job, they have a respectable reason to tell your unfortunate competitor. If you had proffered some unpleasant aspect of your competitor that they accepted, such as their partner not having the required image, they would be in a difficult position in explaining their decision.

Before and perhaps after your presentation you will lobby the decision makers individually, if this is available to you and it is wise to do so. In these meetings, the decision maker may be probing to obtain your insight to any weaknesses of your competitor. This may provide an almost irresistible opportunity for you to denigrate them. Don't do it. It may be a test to see if you can be loyal to your peers. Don't do it anyway. Stick to your non-judgemental comparison of why you would do the job better. If your competitor denigrates you in their own lobbying for the job, you will appear more honourable by comparison. Hopefully that is what the decision makers admire.

Sometimes, opportunities for a step up the ladder may not be foreseen by you and your peers in the organisation. It is important for you to stand back from your position every so often and try to see what changes are in process. 'Keep your ears to the ground.' 'Try to read between the lines.' Speculate on what is happening. Even if you make wrong suppositions you will be alerting yourself to the little changes and unusual circumstances occurring around you. Keep in close contact with the informal centres of influence (see Chapter 8). They will often know things you don't – knowledge that could be beneficial to you.

Summary

As executives rise in the corporate hierarchy, they attain more power. How they exercise it strongly impacts on their image. They should use it in a way that will not damage the self-esteem of those affected.

With power comes decision making – often a source of criticism. The executive who deals with criticism openly and without taking offence gains in image.

Decision making often results in conflict. Treating conflict as a natural dynamic of the decision-making process and controlling the process so that egos are not damaged and interpersonal respect is maintained in reaching a decision is a valuable skill in the arsenal of the executive, and one that is extremely positive to their image.

8

Image and organisational culture

'Image' does not exist in a vacuum. Your image is how others in your organisation value and judge you. And each organisation has its own value system – part of its distinctive culture. You cannot develop and manage your image in your particular organisation without a thorough appreciation of your organisation's culture.

Different cultures/different image

Each organisation has its own distinct culture. Elements of organisational culture include: activities that give it meaning and uniqueness; rules; values; history; hierarchical structure; leadership behaviour; expectations of members' contributions; reward systems; etc. These elements work together to direct and control behaviour and interaction between members within the organisation. The evaluation by others of a member's behaviour and their interaction with fellow members against the background of the organisation's particular culture establishes their image. So an organisation's culture determines what its ideal image should be. Since different organisations have different cultures, they have different ideas on what type of image is appropriate for their organisation.

This can be obvious when comparing organisations in different industries. The image appropriate for an executive in the creative department of an advertising agency is quite different from that of an executive in a private banking firm. In the same industry, cultures tend to be similar. This is because they have the same market, shared training, interchange of members, overseeing industry associations and standards, etc. But there still are differences, if not so obvious. The executive aspiring to success needs to be sensitive to how cultures vary because this insight will indicate why a certain image is more appropriate for any particular organisation.

Cultures can also vary intra-organisationally. The larger the organisation the more likely it is to be structured along different functional or departmental lines, eg corporate planning, human resources, marketing, production, research, financial, information technology, etc. Each of these sub-groups will have its own culture. (Sometimes, even in the same organisation, these sub-groups' cultures can vary so much that they are antagonistic towards each other.) It is not just that these groups utilise specialised knowledge, they may also have different and conflicting value systems. An executive aspiring to general management, and wanting experience in the different functional areas, should assess their ability, and willingness, to operate successfully in widely diverse cultures before taking on the challenge.

Image considerations for new organisational members

An executive considering joining an organisation should research its culture in order to determine the best image to adapt. This requires reading as much as possible about the organisation from its publications and any press articles.

However, the best research is to talk to existing members and ex-members. This should give you enough knowledge to adapt the appropriate image during your application interview. Of course, you will also learn much about the organisation's culture from the person interviewing you.

If your application is successful and you decide the culture is suited to you and you take the job, don't assume that your initial assessment of the culture is entirely correct. It probably won't be. So during the early stages, the best strategy is to be as low-profile and conservative as you can until you are sure about what is the correct image to adopt. Perhaps you may find that an outgoing, assertive image is what's wanted. Well, then you can change to the appropriate behaviour easily enough from your initial conservative stance. But it would be very difficult going from a forceful persona to a conservative one if that was what was required.

The early stages of employment are fundamentally important to a new employee for their behaviour will be closely, although covertly, scrutinised by every organisation member with whom they come into contact. Even those who don't interact with the new member will want to know 'what the new person is like'. First impressions are so important, because they are very difficult to correct. If the image you project is wrong it is the one conveyed around the organisation.

I once worked for an organisation that would introduce new members of staff generally to organisation members at drinks after work finished on a Friday night. The new person was encouraged to say something about their background and interests. On one occasion a new junior executive when introduced said that her interests included 'Sex, drugs and rock and roll'. Most attendees appreciated her humorous self-denigration. However, there were some forced laughs by some of the more senior staff. She turned out to be professional, talented, hard-working and loyal. But it took a long time to get over the image of flippancy she projected on that introduction night.

Aspiring executives will continue to refine their knowledge of the culture and how to function in it. They will learn what image to project in dealing with different levels in the hierarchy and in the different sub-cultures of the organisation. Of course, as their formal role in the organisation changes, they will need to assume an image altered to suit the expectations associated with their new roles. Adapting their image is a continuous process for all executives.

Image and the informal organisation

Up to this point, we have been referring to the 'formal' organisation. A formal organisation is one characterised by organisational charts, lines of authority, titles, written rules, job descriptions, hierarchical levels, status, etc. Behind this visible organisation there are any number of informal organisations. These are loose associations of people who have a common interest outside the daily concerns of the business, eg sporting, religious or cultural interests. They could be open about their activities, eg a theatre-going group, or secretive, eg a drug-using group. The association could be supportive of the formal organisation, eg social club, or potentially in conflict, eg trade union, but most of these groups will be organisationally apolitical, eg supporters of a particular football club. These groups can overlap with common members and through these 'nodal' members information, particularly gossip, can be exchanged and spread quickly throughout the organisation.

It is important for you to identify these 'nodal' members. Some of these will be members of several informal groups. Because of their importance to the flow of informal information these people are often important 'centres of influence'. They can have an incredible amount of informal power and their influence can be surprisingly far-reaching across the organisation and vertically within the hierarchy. Obviously, it is essential that you identify these people and keep them favourably disposed to you. Unexpectedly, in many organisations the receptionist, because of their control of information and general interpersonal skills, may be one of these 'centres of influence'.

Aspiring executives need to be aware of the informal organisations embedded in the more visible structure. They may offer opportunities for enhancing their image. Assume, for instance, there is a group of golfers who regularly play together. This group may be quite diverse with members from all sections and levels of the organisation. Members may include executives of high status whom you would usually never encounter in your daily work. You may have the chance to play with these people. Possibly one of them could take you on in a mentoring capacity, which could be of enormous long-term benefit to you. You need to be careful. Although these groups have fun as an objective, and may exhibit relaxed behaviour, eg they may drink together at the 19th hole, they still may have their own idiosyncratic or unwritten rules, eg inebriation or sexual jokes may be taboo.

Aspiring executives should also beware not to harm their image with the informal groups of which they are members. These groups have their own identities and values that their members protect. Attacking them, even gently mocking them, could cause offence, which will result in a reaction. You may be described in derogatory terms. This branding may be communicated throughout the informal system and your image will suffer.

Summary

You cannot effectively 'sell yourself' in an organisation, you cannot know what is the optimal image to project, unless you have an accurate understanding of the organisation's culture.

Cultures not only vary between organisations, but each organisation may have different cultures in different areas of its operation.

Also, an important consideration in 'selling yourself' is a knowledge of, and sensitivity to, the informal organisations nestled within the more obvious formal structure. These can be important for communicating your image. In particular you must be wary of their 'nodal' centres of influence.

Exercise

The following activities are not only intended to revise the concepts just covered. They are a necessary part of the process of 'Selling Yourself' within your organisation.

1. List five unwritten laws of behaviour in your organisation. (If you cannot identify this many, you are not trying hard enough. Believe me, they are there and you already know them, and more.)

2. List five values that your organisation finds desirable.

3. List the informal groups that you are a member of. List five others that you are not a member of.

4. Identify three organisation members who are centres of influence. For one of them, list the informal groups of which they are a member.

9

Other considerations with image

In all the foregoing it has repeatedly been stressed that an executive's image is determined by others. In successfully 'selling yourself' you can do things to develop, maintain and promote your image but in the end it is something 'owned' by others. Nevertheless, there are aspects of it that are very personal to the executive. These, too, the dedicated executive must take into account when designing and manufacturing an appropriate image.

Your partner's image

Management in organisations is interested in the image of its executives' partners. Senior executives carefully observe the partners to determine whether they are supportive of the organisation and its objectives and whether their behaviour is appropriate in social gatherings and whether they project a 'good' image. If the partners of aspiring executives are seen as having the same values as their partner's, it reflects favourably on the executives' own image.

The senior management also observe to determine if the relationships between executives/managers and their partners are stable and secure. Senior executives do not want aspiring executives to be distracted by relationship breakdown or personal problems associated with their relationships. They want those relationships to be strong and committed. In particular they don't want their aspiring executives to be having office affairs with all the attendant dramas, as covered above.

Senior executives also scrutinise the image of their executives' partners to judge whether, when accompanying those executives, they will project an image consistent with what the organisation wants. If the partner's image is the 'correct' one, the executive's own image will be supported.

Very rarely, if ever, do executives choose their partners with a consideration that their partner's image is appropriate for their own image in their organisation. However, there tends to be a match in most cases, for the values and judgements involved in commitment to an organisation are similar to those involved in commitment to a partner; if the executive 'fits', the partner probably will too.

If you feel that the image of your partner is not the one desired by your organisation you have a few alternatives. You could change organisations to one better suited to your partner, although the new one may also not like their image. You could change your partner to one more suitable, or you could try to change your partner's image. More realistically, you could just make do.

This does not mean doing nothing. You need to be sensitive to how and when your partner's image might reflect negatively on you and avoid the opportunities for this happening. Often, your partner, sensitive to your situation, can be encouraged to refrain from any offending behaviour. However, if this is not possible, organise circumstances so that you are not exposed to any threat.

Remedies for a damaged image

What you can do if you have seriously damaged your image

If you like your organisation and are willing to work on improving your image, you could talk to your manager/supervisor and, if the organisation is big enough, arrange a transfer to another department or another geographical area where your previous image is not that relevant.

The difficulty in attempting to improve a damaged image *in situ* is that a bad impression is amazingly persistent. Not only do people hold onto negative beliefs concerning others, they will tend to interpret contrary evidence in such a way that it will support their disapproving opinions. Any efforts in self-promotion might be wasted or, even, counterproductive.

You need a 'champion'; someone who will publicly support you; someone held in high esteem in the organisation; someone who is psychologically strong enough to be prepared to defend you against popular, derogatory opinion. This may be an important person in the formal structure. Their goodwill towards you will be noticed by others and, because of respect for their position, their support may be influential over time in changing the prevalent negative judgement. However, because they are concerned about their own image in associating with you, it might be hard to find someone sympathetic.

However, there are also individuals in the informal structure who hold great influence. These tend to be longer-term employees who have reached a plateau of responsibility. They generally have a great deal of organisational experience; they are the ones 'who know how the organisation works'. These people are well liked, respected and non-threatening. They are identifiable because people go to them for advice – the organisational 'Wise Owls'.

You may not be able to immediately befriend such an individual but you can use them as a channel to communicate to the organisation that you have decided to alter the behaviour that has damaged your image. If you are sincere, the 'Wise Owl' may give you a sympathetic ear, which will be noted by your detractors and which may stimulate the start of an attitudinal change in your favour.

Gender differences with image

Most women feel disadvantaged in the managerial workplace dominated by men. The stereotypical leader/manager is male, and staff of both genders are generally more accustomed to being managed by men. Some feel uncomfortable with women in a position of control. Women managers are sensitive to these issues. Obviously they would prefer that their gender was not a dimension to their image, and in the ideal world it should not be that way, but it is still a fact that women have to pay more attention to their image than men.

The obvious area in which they have to be careful is not to use their sexual appeal in the management of men. This can be quite difficult. All their lives this has been a component in their interaction with men. It may even be such a natural part of their dealing with men that they may not be aware of how they take advantage of their sexuality. Turning it off may first require their awareness of its ever-present dimension.

It does not work the other way. Men are not disapproved of if they have charm and use it with the other sex in getting the job done. But women are judged unfairly if they take advantage of their feminine appeal.

The woman manager needs to maintain the appropriate professional image, and simultaneously her need to suppress any unintentional non-verbal message that might be misinterpreted requires constant alertness. Similarly she must be vigilant that she does not overcompensate and be perceived as aloof or cold or unfeminine. Achieving just the right image is more stressful for the woman manager than a man in a similar position because of this gender dynamic.

The problems that she experiences cannot readily be shared with other organisational members. Obviously not with men, but also not with other women with whom she may be, or come to be, in competition and who might use the information of any 'weakness' against her. The solution is to network with female executives from other organisations with whom she can share experiences and discuss situational difficulties and enjoy mutual support.

Image changes with age

Society's expectations about how its elder members should behave are reflected in the variations to image that organisations expect from its older executives. These variations are not negative in most organisations. Older executives are expected to be mature, thoughtful, supportive, experienced, risk-averse and canny. Many successful organisations ensure that a significant component of their management team is made up of older more experienced executives who may provide, in strategic decision making, a balance to more impulsive/aggressive elements.

There are some organisations whose cultures promote a more dynamic, risk-taking environment. Such organisations are usually young themselves or may fail before they reach maturity. If they do survive, their cultures change to become more accepting and appreciative of the inputs from more experienced executives.

An executive's ability to manipulate their image to match the needs of the organisation diminishes to some extent with age. No matter how dynamic their personalities are, or how aggressive their temperaments, expectations about executives based on age will gradually overtake their ability to project the 'youthful' image if that is what is required. If the organisation cannot appreciate the inputs from its experienced executives, the elder executive is better finding a position with one that does.

Image versus personal style

This book promotes the idea that an executive's image can be
moulded and managed to suit the culture of the organisation they
are working in. Success is more readily achieved to the extent that
the executives have made a good fit between how they are
perceived and what the organisation wants.

The Machiavellian concept that executives should cynically
manipulate their actual personalities to fit some organisation
ideal is not what is intended, nor is it possible in reality. It is
possible to adapt behaviour, we do it all the time often
subconsciously, eg we speak in hushed tones in churches or
libraries. But adapting behaviour is not the same as changing our
inner selves.

This book encourages executives to be aware of their
behaviour and how it impacts on their image and to choose or
reject behaviour on the basis of whether it enhances or damages
that image. This awareness and behaviour modification may veil
your 'real' personality for a short period, hopefully during that
initial period when your organisational image is developing and
you are establishing the 'good' image you are after. Eventually the
'real' you will present itself. If you have unattractive components
in your make-up, your self-awareness and the good habits that
have become ingrained in your dealings with others should
reduce much of the negative impact. More positively, most of us
are likeable, or mainly so, and as this aspect of us becomes
apparent it will add to the good image we have striven to project.

For a short period in my early career I was a high-school
teacher. I had no specific training in teaching and my head teacher
told me that from the start I should be cold, distant, humourless,
professional and aloof with my students who were not much
younger than I was at the time. Later, having established an image
as a serious and mature teacher, I could, he said, allow myself to
be friendlier and enjoy the experience. He was so right. I took his
advice and thoroughly enjoyed the experience and, I believe,
contributed to my students' education. Had I been as relaxed,

open and amiable at the start as I was later to become, I would never had established the suitable and effective image and gained the respect to do my job, yet I would have had the same knowledge of the subject matter I was teaching.

First job – new job

The implications from this are obvious. The most effective time to design and manufacture your image is in the early stages of your employment. Your fellow workers have no previous behaviour on which to assess you, so you can promote yourself more or less as you like. It is also in the early stages, as they are getting to know you, that they are scrutinising you closely. You may not even be aware they are doing so, but they are. As an unknown, they consider you either as a threat or an opportunity for them. In this state they are very impressionable. It is a great opportunity for you to establish yourself in their eyes in the best possible light.

Once you have made a good impression, any slip in your standards will be treated more leniently (but they will not be forever forgiving). It does not work the other way. If you exhibit undesired behaviour before you establish a good image, then you won't be able to establish a good image as quickly or as efficiently. You will have lost your opportunity. So be very careful in the early stages. Your eventual success may very well depend on it.

Summary

Your image is not totally in your control to manipulate. You would not/cannot change your age, gender, partner, personality, length of time with your organisation. Nevertheless these dimensions can impact on your image and your ability to sell yourself effectively. By appreciating their interaction with your image, you can minimise any unwanted outcomes.

10

Conclusion

Most business executives start their careers with the driving ambition to climb the corporate ladder as far, and as quickly, as they can. They think that by pouring their efforts into doing their job as well as possible, success will come their way as a matter of course. When it doesn't they are frustrated and disillusioned.

Even those who have progressed some way in achieving their goals have a feeling that they might have done better. To get as far up as they have, they may have had an innate understanding of the usefulness of projecting an appropriate image. Or, they may have observed others who were successful and developed a vague idea of how to go about self-promotion. Yet there is the feeling they might have gone further.

You, the reader, no matter where you are in your career path, now know better.

You know that success is intimately tied to the image others have of you. You know what to do to promote your image and protect it on an ongoing basis. You know how to conduct yourself in the work environment to maximise you advancement.

But knowing how is nothing. Unless you put that knowledge to work for you.

It's now up to you to SELL YOURSELF.

Appendix 1

Principal concepts presented in this book

- 'Image' is not what you are. It is what others think you are.
- Every time you communicate with others you project an image.
- A 'good' image is only partly dependant on how well you do your job.
- By habitually demonstrating certain Success Indicators you can project a 'good' image. The basis of most of these is respect for others.
- Apart from these Success Indicators that everyone wants to see in you, people of different status need something special for their needs.
- Repeated self-assessment is necessary to develop an understanding of what you are doing well or wrong.
- The best skill to acquire for 'selling yourself' is public speaking.
- 'Selling yourself' is a never-ending process. The higher you go up the corporate ladder the more complex this selling becomes.
- Understanding the culture of your organisation and its informal structure is a necessary prerequisite for successfully 'selling yourself'.

Appendix 2

A suggested plan for starting the process of 'selling yourself'

At the end of some of the chapters above, there have been recommendations given for putting into practice the concepts covered in those sections. This Appendix pulls these together into a composite plan.

The first considerations of a plan are: What are your objectives that you want from your work commitment? and, What are your personal resources you bring to the job? In this situation, these both intimately involve YOU.

How you answer these questions is a very personal affair and you will conduct it in your own way. To get satisfying answers is difficult. It might be disappointing. Not because of what it reveals to you about you, but because you realise you have never put yourself through the process before in a disciplined manner. You might find out that you have been working with only a nebulous idea of what you truly want to achieve.

All I can recommend is that you accept that you have not carried out this self-evaluation unless you provide answers to these questions WRITTEN DOWN. It is no use just to think about them. They won't crystallise in your mind until you can write them down. This way they can be reviewed honestly in the future and you can measure your progress.

The ancient Greek aphorism 'Know Thyself', is one of the most difficult philosophical directives, but also the most constructive. It is not easy, but, heck, it is your life. If you don't know what you bring to your life, and what you want out of it, don't be surprised if you feel a sense of ennui and dissatisfaction.

So much for the sermonising. Having written the answers down you can now start the plan to 'sell yourself' in your organisation.

There is no best way of going through the process but the following suggestions might help:

- **Read Chapter 8 on Organisational Culture. Now write down (don't just think about it) what constitutes the core values of your organisation. What does it expect of its members? What is the 'Corporate Man' for your organisation? Take your time. Subconsciously you know the answers. It is just that they may never have been explicitly stated to you. But you have learned them by a kind of social osmosis. It might help to choose someone who, in your organisation, exemplifies the ideal executive and analyse what it is about them that makes them a role model. List their qualities.**
- **Now consider the Success Indicators listed in Chapter 2. Are these valid for your organisation? Does your chosen role model exhibit them? If so, these are components of the image you want to promote in your organisation. Again write them down.**
- **Now look at Chapter 4 and those behaviours that can damage your good image. Are you guilty of such behaviour? Which ones? Write them down.**
- **Now, with reference to Chapter 3, assess how well you provide for the needs of organisational members in their various status levels. Looking at the table at the end of the chapter, what can you do that you are not presently**

doing? Or what can you do better? Write down your conclusions.
- Read Chapter 6. Which ideas in this chapter apply to you? If nothing else, if you are not a polished pubic speaker, plan to do an appropriate course. Or join an organisation such as Toastmasters.

You have gathered all the input you need for your plan.

All plans need objectives. Ideally these must be quantifiable and measurable and they must have timeframes in which to achieve them. If your objective is to 'sell yourself' and to do it well, how do you know if you have been successful and to what extent? You cannot measure the quality of your image on a scale.

And you can't exactly seek feedback from others. If you were to say, for instance, 'How well do you think my image is coming along?' you may get an embarrassed evasive reply, like, 'Oh you're doing all right, I think.' More likely you will get a look of puzzlement. Remember, most people never consider their image as something that requires ongoing attention. You may from time-to-time get some unexpected feedback, maybe the occasional compliment, or reference to your image during a performance review. But not enough feedback to measure objectives against.

Since this is the case, you are forced to make subjective evaluations on your progress, with all the potential pitfalls of self-evaluation, especially self-delusion.

It is better, I think, to list all the things you want to do that you know from your reading will boost your image and to review regularly whether you are carrying them out. These activities that you set yourself mean a change in behaviour. Behaviour will not change without frequent reviews and re-commitment. The activities that you want to introduce on a daily basis need review daily. This is why I have suggested evaluating yourself either on your way to work or coming home. It can quickly develop into a habit and with your repeated, frequent attention your behaviour will change. Say, for example, you decide that an activity you wish to adopt is to give a cheery greeting to those you work with each morning. Asking yourself daily whether you have done so will soon result with your doing it habitually.

So your plan could be a list of activities you want to carry out. Activities that you want to carry out daily should be reviewed daily. Longer term activities/behavioural changes such as responding appropriately to criticism, should be reviewed less regularly, say weekly. But you must have a plan that says when all these activities are going to be reviewed and then stick to it.

The whole process and particularly performing the reviews on schedule needs discipline but, if you really want to 'sell yourself' well, you will do it.

The wonderful thing is that devising the plan is a huge achievement in itself because in producing it you have so focused on your image and ways to improve it that behaving in a way that will promote a 'good' image will start to become second nature to you. And the longer the plan is in effect, the more sensitive you will become to issues of image.

Creating Success series

The above titles are available from all good bookshops.
For further information on these and other Kogan Page titles, or to
order online, visit the Kogan Page website at
www.koganpage.com